able of Contents

All terms appearing in boldfaced type in the text are defined in the Glossary that appears on page 64.

*J*apan is an island country in eastern Asia. It is made up of four large islands and many smaller ones. In fact, if you counted up all the islands that belonged to Japan, there would be almost 4000! As an island country, Japan is surrounded on all sides by water. The two biggest bodies of water around Japan are the Sea of Japan to the west and the Pacific Ocean to the east.

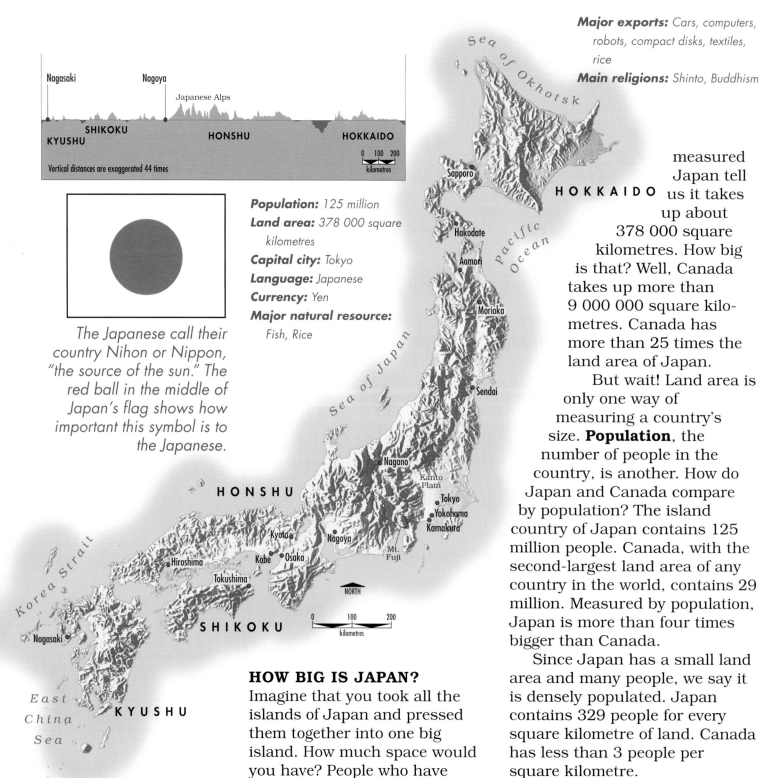

Major exports: Cars, computers, robots, compact disks, textiles, rice

Main religions: Shinto, Buddhism

Nagasaki   Nagoya

Japanese Alps

KYUSHU   SHIKOKU   HONSHU   HOKKAIDO

0   100   200
kilometres

Vertical distances are exaggerated 44 times

Population: 125 million
Land area: 378 000 square kilometres
Capital city: Tokyo
Language: Japanese
Currency: Yen
Major natural resource: Fish, Rice

The Japanese call their country Nihon or Nippon, "the source of the sun." The red ball in the middle of Japan's flag shows how important this symbol is to the Japanese.

measured Japan tell us it takes up about 378 000 square kilometres. How big is that? Well, Canada takes up more than 9 000 000 square kilometres. Canada has more than 25 times the land area of Japan.

But wait! Land area is only one way of measuring a country's size. **Population**, the number of people in the country, is another. How do Japan and Canada compare by population? The island country of Japan contains 125 million people. Canada, with the second-largest land area of any country in the world, contains 29 million. Measured by population, Japan is more than four times bigger than Canada.

Since Japan has a small land area and many people, we say it is densely populated. Japan contains 329 people for every square kilometre of land. Canada has less than 3 people per square kilometre.

HOW BIG IS JAPAN?
Imagine that you took all the islands of Japan and pressed them together into one big island. How much space would you have? People who have

Japan: Where Is It?

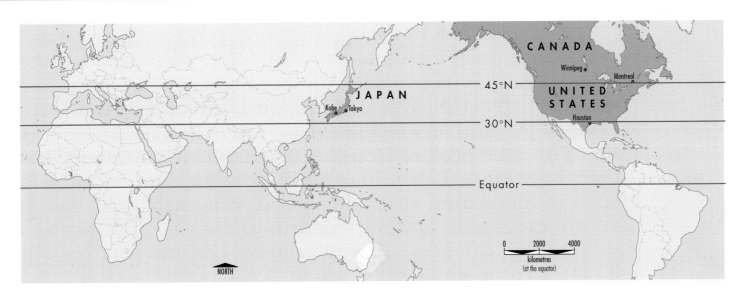

CLIMATE

The country of Japan is very long. It is so long that it contains three different climate areas: north, central, and south. Look at the map above. You can see that the northernmost part of Japan is almost on the same **latitude** as Montreal, Quebec (Latitude measures distance north or south of the equator.) The southernmost part is almost on the same latitude as Houston, Texas. In northern Japan there is lots of snow in the winter, and the summer is short and mild. In central Japan the climate is **temperate**. Here the winter is not too cold and the summer is not uncomfortably hot. Southern Japan has a **subtropical** climate. Summers are hot and long. It rarely gets cold in the winter. In fact, the average winter temperature is 16°C. This region is also very wet. In September **typhoons** or tropical storms bring heavy rainfall and high winds. The power of the winds can damage houses and other buildings. The rains often result in floods that cause further damage.

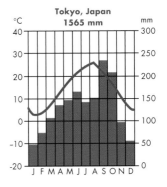

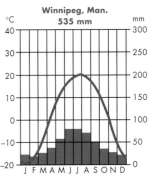

The two graphs show how the climate of Tokyo, Japan differs from that of Winnipeg, Canada. The line in each graph shows the temperature, and the bars show the average rain- or snowfall. What is the hottest month in Winnipeg? In Tokyo? What month has the highest rainfall in each place? Can you guess why the rainfall is so high in Tokyo in this month?

SOMETHING TO DO

1. Think, pair, square. We have seen that Japan is an island country and is densely populated. Choose a partner and brainstorm the following questions. Then meet with another pair of students and share your answers.

   a. There are good and bad things about living on an island. The good things are called advantages, and the bad things disadvantages. Make a two-column organizer on a piece of paper. In the first column list the advantages in living on an island. In the second column list the disadvantages. (Hint: Would it be easy or hard for another country to invade Japan?)

   b. Since there are so many people in Japan, some things are in short supply and very expensive to buy. Make a list of things you think would be more expensive in Japan than in Canada. (Hint: Would houses be cheaper in Japan or Canada?) Explain your reasons.

2. The climate of Japan changes from north to south. Nagasaki is at 32° latitude and Sapporo is at 43° latitude. Which city will be hotter in the summer? Why?

3

In addition to being an island country, Japan is also very mountainous. In fact, more than 70% of the country is covered with mountains or high hills. The highest mountain in Japan is called **Fujisan** (Foo-jee-san) in Japanese. In English it is known as Mount Fuji. The peak of Mount Fuji is so high it is covered in snow year round. To the Japanese people, Mount Fuji is a symbol of the beauty of their country. It is more than just a beautiful mountain, however. Mount Fuji is also a **volcano**, a mountain that can send up explosions of gas and fiery rock. It last erupted almost 300 years ago, in 1707.

Many Japanese artists have painted pictures of Mount Fuji. Each summer people come from all over Japan to climb to the top of this mountain. Most take a bus part of the way, then walk the rest. On a nice summer day there can be as many as 25 000 people climbing Mount Fuji.

Since Mount Fuji's last eruption was so long ago, it is called a **dormant** or sleeping volcano. Scientists are not sure whether it will erupt again. Volcanoes that have been dormant for a thousand years are called **extinct**. This means they will never erupt again.

Some volcanoes in Japan are still **active**. They can erupt at any time. If they are close to a populated area, these volcanoes can cause much damage and cost many lives. Around the world there are about 500 active volcanoes, but only about 25 erupt each year. In Japan there are about 200 volcanoes. More than 60 of them are active.

Geologists are scientists who study the earth. Using very sensitive equipment, they listen for signs of the next volcanic eruption so that the people who live in that area can be warned. When the earth rumbles, that is a signal that a volcano may be about to erupt.

WHY DO VOLCANOES HAPPEN?

As you can see in the map on page 6, the earth's crust is divided into large sections called **plates**. These plates are in constant motion, but they move so slowly no one can feel it. Most volcanoes begin close to where two plates meet. The grinding of one plate against another can cause a **fault** or crack to appear in one of the plates. Through this crack, **magma** or liquid rock pushes to the surface.

When magma breaks through the crust of the earth it is called **lava**. When a volcano erupts, lava shoots out of the **central vent** or main passageway along

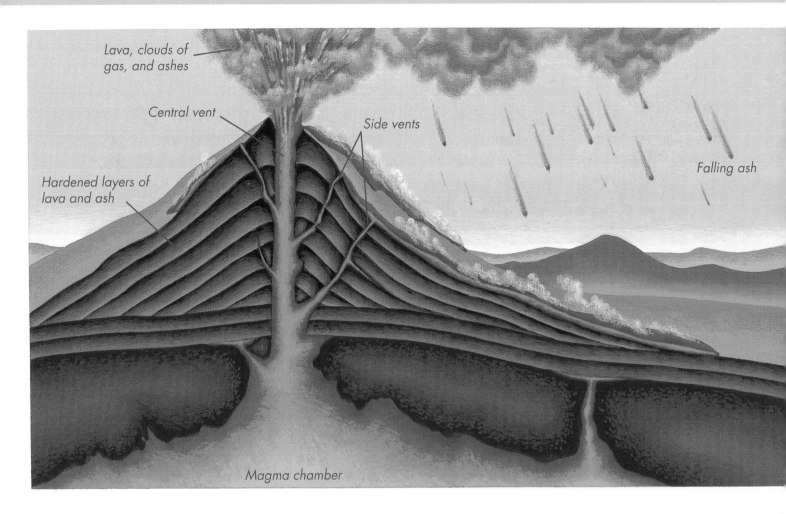

Lava, clouds of gas, and ashes

Central vent

Side vents

Falling ash

Hardened layers of lava and ash

Magma chamber

with ash and gas. Sometimes a volcano has other openings. Eruptions can occur at these side vents too. Lava runs like water down the volcano's **cone** or mountain and can cause a lot of harm. Anything that gets in the way of a lava flow will burn up and then be buried in the lava stream.

SOMETHING TO DO

1. With other members of your class, role-play the following scene. Mount Fuji is about to erupt for the first time in 300 years. You are part of the Japanese television news team assigned to cover this story. You will need the following people:

   - a news anchor to broadcast the story.
   - an on-site reporter to interview the following people:
     - a person who lives near Mount Fuji.
     - a person who has come from another part of Japan to climb Mount Fuji.
     - a geologist, who is predicting when Mount Fuji will erupt and how damaging the eruption will be.
     - a scientist explaining with charts how a volcano works.
     - a government official, who is telling how many people will have to be evacuated and what safety precautions to take.

   Students who are not playing the roles themselves can help write the scripts for each character.

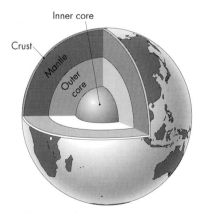

Inner core

Crust

Mantle

Outer core

The earth's interior is divided into four major zones. The inner core is solid rock and the outer core is liquid rock. The mantle is made up mostly of solid rock but also contains some liquid rock or magma. The outer layer is called the crust.

apan is often rocked by **earthquakes** or shakings of the earth's surface. Some earthquakes are so small they can't even be felt by humans. Others are strong enough to heave the ground up violently, tossing cars and buildings about as if they were toys.

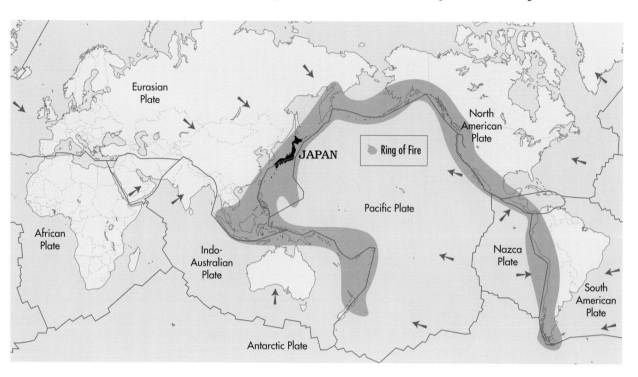

The plates of the earth's crust. The Ring of Fire is an area around the Pacific Ocean where many earth-quakes and volcanoes occur. The arrows show in which direction the plates are moving.

Eurasian Plate

North American Plate

JAPAN

Ring of Fire

Pacific Plate

African Plate

Indo-Australian Plate

Nazca Plate

South American Plate

Antarctic Plate

The Kobe earthquake twisted and toppled the Hanshin Expressway.

A major earthquake rocked Japan on January 17, 1995. The quake's **epicentre** (the place where it first reached the earth's surface) was about 100 km from the city of Kobe and registered 7.2 on the Richter scale. (Anything over 7.0 is considered major.) The quake killed more than 6000 people and damaged more than 100 000 houses. It twisted railroad tracks into crazy loops and threw an entire high-way overpass to the ground. People who lived in the hardest-hit parts of the city had to go without running water and gas for heating and cooking for months.

People around the world offered generous donations of time, money, clothing, and household goods to victims of the Kobe earthquake. Many

buildings, highways, and train lines were rebuilt within a few months. To the rest of the world, it seemed as if Kobe recovered quickly from the damage. To the people of Kobe, however, the effects of the disaster lasted much longer. Some survivors lost their homes, workplaces, family members, and friends. They had to collect their remaining belong-ings and go to live in schools, sports arenas, and community centres.

Months later, small pre-made houses were opened for the elderly and disabled, but everyone else had to move in with relatives or find new homes on their own. With so many people looking for a new place to live and a new job, more problems followed. In the following months, an additional 800

Plate 1   Epicentre

Plate 2

Shock waves

people died, most of them from injuries suffered earlier. A year later, the mayor of Kobe said, "It will take five more years to finish rebuilding, and another 10 to 20 years to heal all the wounds."

In Japan, many houses are still made of wood and built close together. Most homes still use small kerosene or gas heaters. For these reasons, fire spreads quickly. In fact, most of the damage after any quake comes from fire and **tsunami** (tsoo-nah-mee). These are huge sea waves that are set in motion by the heaving up of the ocean floor during a quake.

Since quakes occur so often in Japan, children must do earthquake drills at school. They practice getting under their desks or tables and putting on special helmets. It is very difficult to stand up in a bad quake, so the children must move quickly. Japanese scientists, politicians, and citizens are trying hard to prepare for future earthquakes. Quakes are difficult to predict, so many scientists from around the world have decided to share their research.

They hope that through international cooperation more lives can be saved.

As you can see in the map on page 6, the earth's crust is made up of a number of plates. These are huge sections of crust that slowly push against each other. Pressure builds up wherever two plates meet. This pressure causes the earth to shake, creating an earthquake. The scraping of plates against each other also creates magma. This liquid rock rises through the earth's surface, forming volcanic mountains. Japan lies right at the point where three plates meet. This explains why there are so many earthquakes and volcanoes in Japan.

Houses were crushed like cardboard boxes by the Kobe quake.

SOMETHING TO DO

1. Find the words in this chapter that mean:
   a. The centre of an earthquake.
   b. A large sea wave.

2. Explain to a partner how the big Kobe earthquake changed the lives of people in Kobe. How do you think the earthquake survivors felt at the time of the quake? The day after the quake? A year after the quake?

Samurai (sam-uh-ry) were much like the European knights of the Middle Ages. They were tough, well-trained warriors who swore to fight to the death for their lord. Instead of the code of chivalry, the samurai followed **bushido** (boosh-ee-doh), the "way of the warrior." They believed that values such as courage, honour, and loyalty were more important than life itself.

The shape of society in feudal Japan. Feudalism lasted in Japan from about 1100 to 1868.

Emperor

Shogun

Daimyo and other nobility

Samurai warriors

Craftspeople, merchants, and peasants

THE FEUDAL SYSTEM

The samurai began as bands of warriors roaming the countryside. After a time each band came under the control of the most powerful noble in the area. A noble with many samurai at his command was called a **daimyo** (dime-yoh). In return for a samurai's loyalty, the daimyo gave him land and protection. Just as the samurai swore to be loyal to a daimyo, the daimyo had to swear loyalty to the **shogun** (show-gun). The shogun was the military leader under the emperor, who was ruler of all Japan.

This kind of society is called a **feudal system**. It is divided into different levels. People in each level pledge to serve those in the level directly above them. In return, they are given land and protection. If you drew a picture of a feudal society, it would be something like a pyramid in shape. There would be a few very powerful people at the top and many poor people at the bottom. On page 8 is a diagram of Japanese society during feudal times.

BUSHIDO

The key part of bushido, the samurai code, was loyalty to the daimyo or lord. Other virtues were also important, such as honesty and humility. Most of all, a good samurai had to practice the martial arts and be absolutely fearless in battle.

Samurai practiced fighting with a number of weapons. The most important of these was the sword. When a young samurai turned 15, he was given his first sword in a special ceremony. Every samurai carried two swords, one short and one long. The long sword had to be sharp and strong enough to cut off an opponent's head with one blow. The steel blade of the sword was made very carefully by skilled swordsmiths. It was folded and pounded flat 100 times and then honed until it was sharp as a razor.

In battle, a samurai would also fight with a bow and arrow and a long spear. If all his weapons were taken from him, a warrior still had to be able to defend himself. This is why the samurai practiced the art of **karate**, which in Japanese means "empty hand." A samurai who was defeated in battle usually killed himself. He believed this was the only way to save his honour.

SAMURAI ARTS

The samurai did not spend all their time fighting or training for battle. They believed it was also important to practice different arts. Each of the arts the samurai practiced had very strict rules. They all stressed the virtue of **simplicity** and the beauty of the natural world. These arts included the tea ceremony, flower arranging, and poetry.

Basho, the greatest **haiku** (high-koo) poet in Japan, was a samurai warrior. On the death of his lord, Basho put away his armour and weapons and became a wandering poet. He was very poor, but by the time Basho died he had written hundreds of poems. These poems are still read and admired by the Japanese people today.

*A samurai's armour was specially designed to be lightweight but offer protection against swords and arrows. It was made of many small iron plates joined together. His helmet had horns to scare the enemy. Before battle, a samurai burned **incense** in his helmet. This way his head would smell sweet if his enemy cut it off. On the back of his armour, each samurai wore a small coloured banner with a symbol that identified his family. This banner was called a **sashimono** (sah-shee-moh-noh). It showed which side he was on in the confusion of battle.*

SOMETHING TO DO

1. A samurai wears a sashimono or coloured banner on his back to identify his family. Create your own banner on a piece of material. Choose material that is in your favourite colour and design a symbol to represent your family.

2. If you could go back in time to feudal Japan, what level of society would you like to live in? Explain why.

*A crow sits
On a withered tree
This autumn evening.
—Basho (1644-1694)*

y the 1930s Japan had become a powerful nation. The country had many modern factories and a powerful army. At the same time, there were serious problems in Japan. Because of the large population, food shortages and high unemployment rates were common. Japanese industries needed more **raw materials,** such as coal and iron ore, for their factories. Military leaders decided to invade nearby countries. They thought this would give Japan greater supplies of food and raw materials and make it a stronger country. Other nations resisted Japan's plans, and soon a great war developed. This became known as World War II.

In their attack on Pearl Harbor on December 7, 1941, the Japanese sank or seriously damaged 18 warships and destroyed or damaged more than 200 aircraft. More than 3000 U.S. soldiers were killed in the attack.

Only a few buildings remained standing after the atom bomb hit Hiroshima. This building is called the Atom Bomb Dome. Today it is a memorial for people who died from the bomb.

SURPRISE ATTACK!

At first the Japanese armies won many battles. In a surprise attack on the United States Navy at Pearl Harbor, Japanese air planes destroyed a large part of the U.S. fleet. By 1942, Japan controlled much of Southeast Asia and many islands in the Pacific Ocean. Then the tide began to turn. From 1942 to 1945, the United States won several naval battles with Japan and took back many of the Pacific islands. Soon the U.S. had air fields within range of Japan and began bombing raids over Japan's major cities and industrial centres.

In spite of the terrible loss of life from these air raids, Japan's military leaders did not want to surrender. The U.S. and other nations prepared to invade Japan. In the meantime, scientists in the United States had developed a new weapon, the **atomic bomb**. An atomic bomb creates a huge explosion by releasing nuclear energy instead of the high explosives in other bombs.

Leaders in the U.S. warned that if Japan did not surrender this new kind of bomb would be dropped on a Japanese city. No surrender was announced, and on August 6, 1945, the first atomic bomb was dropped on Hiroshima, killing more than 70 000 people in one terrible explosion. Three days later another atomic bomb was dropped on Nagasaki. Shortly afterwards the emperor announced Japan's surrender and World War II was over.

CHANGES TO JAPANESE SOCIETY

After the war, the United States army occupied Japan. During this period several major changes occurred in Japanese society.

- Instead of an **imperial government** ruled by an emperor, Japan became a **democracy**. This means the people were able to choose their leaders by voting. The Emperor became a symbolic leader with no real power.

- For the first time in Japanese history, women were allowed to vote. Women enjoyed other new rights, including the right to own property.

- Japan had to give up its army and weapons and promise not to invade other countries.

- **Land reforms** took big farms from a few rich landholders and divided them up among individual farmers.

By 1956, only 11 years after the end of the war, Japan's economy had recovered. This small country was on its way to becoming one of the wealthiest nations in the world.

SADAKO AND THE THOUSAND CRANES

On the summer day the atomic bomb was dropped on Hiroshima, about 300 000 people lived in the city. One of them was a two-year-old girl named Sadako. Sadako was not visibly injured by the explosion and she seemed fine for the next 10 years. Then she began to feel weak and dizzy. One day she collapsed at school. Sadako was sent to a special hospital for people who had radiation sickness from the atomic bomb. Doctors discovered Sadako had **leukemia**, a form of cancer. She must have received a dose of radiation when the bomb exploded.

While Sadako was in the hospital, one of her friends came to visit. Japanese children like to fold pieces of paper into shapes that look like different animals. This is called **origami.** Sadako's friend gave her an origami paper crane. She told Sadako that if she folded one thousand cranes, the gods would grant her wish to be healthy again. Sadako tried hard. She managed to fold 644 cranes, but on October 25, 1955, she died. Her classmates finished the cranes and placed them on Sadako's grave.

All of Japan heard Sadako's story. In 1958, a statue of Sadako holding a crane was built in Hiroshima in the Peace Park. Each year on August 6, school children from all over Japan bring their folded cranes to the statue.

SOMETHING TO DO

1. The crane has become a powerful symbol for peace. Can you think of any other peace symbols? Draw as many as you can.

2. Working with a partner, create a poster, poem, or skit that has a message of peace.

he family is a very important part of Japanese society. Traditionally, each member of the family had his or her own duties and responsibilities. Today family roles have changed quite a lot, but there are still set roles for each family member.

This is the Hayashi family. They live just outside Osaka, a port city on the large island of Honshu. Find Osaka on the map on page 2. What kind of climate do you think Osaka has?

Most Japanese families today live in cities. The typical family has a two- or three-bedroom house or apartment. Usually the father works outside the home while the mother cares for the children and manages the family's money. The mother is in charge of the children's education from kindergarten to university. On top of this responsibility, she usually does all the cooking and housework.

In the past, a Japanese child's seventh birthday marked an important change. When boys and girls turned seven, they began to help with household chores and take part in community activities. Today, a child's most important duty is to study hard at school. Success or failure at school will control what children do for the rest of their lives. It will have an effect on what kind of job they get. It may even affect their choice of marriage partners.

The leaders of Japan, both in politics and business, used to be men only. Women were not supposed to have a career and were not supposed to give orders to men. In family life it was the same way. The working man was always the head of an **extended family** of grandparents, parents, and children living together in one house. He made all the important decisions, and his wife had little to say. This began to change over the last 50 years. Married women were given more rights in the new laws that were written. Today they have a greater say in family affairs and in public life.

The Japanese extended family has also changed over the last 50 years. Many young people have moved away from home to go to college or follow their careers. After marrying or finding a good job, they do not want to move back home. As a result, the typical Japanese household today is a **nuclear family** with a mother, father, and two or three children.

THE HAYASHI FAMILY

Noriko Hayashi is 13 years old. Her last name, Hayashi, means "woods" or "small forest." This is what her last name looks like in Japanese characters: 林. She is in grade eight, the second year of junior high school. Noriko began studying English in grade seven like all students in Japan. She also enjoys school club activities such as tennis and **kendo** (fencing with a bamboo stick). Her younger brother Taro is 11 years old. He is in fifth grade at elementary school. Taro likes going to video arcades and playing baseball with his friends after school.

Shingo Hayashi, the children's father, is 45 years old. He is what the Japanese call a **sarariman**. This word comes from the English words "salary man." It means he wears a suit and works in an office for a big company. Mr. Hayashi has a stressful life. He **commutes**, or goes back and forth to work, by train six days a week. The trip takes 90 minutes in each direction. Taro and Noriko hardly ever see their father during the week, because he works late almost every night. After work, Mr. Hayashi often has to spend time entertaining business clients. He does not like spending so much time away from his family, but society expects him to consider work more important.

Yuka Hayashi is 42 years old. She studied accounting in college and worked for six years before getting married. She spends much of her time helping her children with homework, talking to their teachers, preparing meals, doing housework, and organizing the family's finances. She tries to find time to have lunch with friends and study English conversation. Mrs. Hayashi hopes to use her English skills when she travels on vacation with her husband. English will also come in handy if Mrs. Hayashi wants to find a part-time job.

On Sundays, Mr. and Mrs. Hayashi often do something special with Taro and Noriko. They go on a picnic or to an amusement park. Sometimes they visit Mrs. Hayashi's parents or have dinner in a nice restaurant. Sunday is often family day in Japan.

After reading this chapter, look at this picture carefully. Is it a picture of a nuclear family or an extended family? Explain your answer.

SOMETHING TO DO

1. Mr. Hayashi's ride on the commuter train to work takes 90 minutes each way. How many hours does Mr. Hayashi spend on the train in one week?

2. What is your role in your family? Make a list of your duties and compare it with your classmates. Is homework as important for you as it is for Noriko and Taro?

There are many different kinds of homes in Japan. Some people still live in traditional Japanese houses made completely of wood and with tile roofs. Others live in modern apartment buildings made of brick and cement. Most people, though, live in houses or apartments that combine traditional and modern features.

The art and flowers in the tokonoma change as the seasons change.

THE HAYASHIS' HOUSE

The Hayashi family lives in a modern two-storey house. In this neighbourhood, the houses are very close together so the back yards are quite small. In spite of this, Taro still has a garden in the back yard. It contains one tree, some shrubs, and a small space to grow flowers and vegetables. Even in the country-side, the yards and gardens are rather small. Japan has so many people for its size that all of the land is used for something.

The Hayashi house is made of cement and contains little wood. Wood has become very expensive in Japan because most of it is **imported,** or brought in from other countries. Japan is not big enough to grow all the trees it needs for wood products. The Hayashi house has an old-fash-ioned tile roof. Tile roofs are usually slanted. There is so much rain in much of Japan, it is important that the water runs off the roofs easily.

One room of the Hayashi home is a traditional Japanese room, called a **tatami** (tah-tah-mee) room. The floor is covered with tatami mats, which are made from rice straw. Each mat measures one metre by two metres. It takes eight mats to cover the floor in the Hayashis' tatami room. In the corner of the Hayashi's dining room is a **tokonoma** (toh-koh-noh-mah). This is a space in the wall

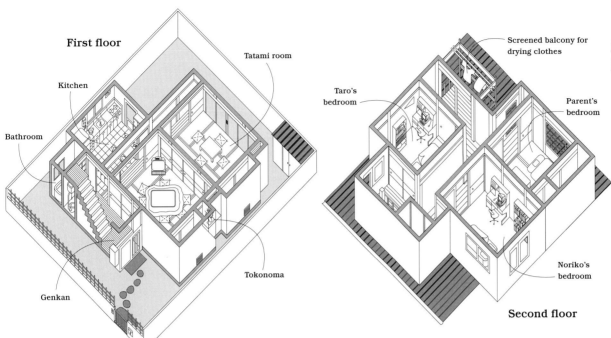

First floor

Tatami room

Kitchen

Bathroom

Genkan

Tokonoma

Screened balcony for drying clothes

Floor plan of the Hayashi home.

Taro's bedroom

Parent's bedroom

Noriko's bedroom

Second floor

shaped like a rectangle. It contains a painted **scroll** or long sheet of paper and a flower arrangement.

The Hayashi home, like most Japanese homes, has a **genkan.** This is a special entrance hall to the house. Here, each person entering the house has to take off his or her shoes and put on a pair of slippers. Except in the tatami room, the house has modern furniture. The kitchen contains several electrical appliances, including a rice cooker, a stove, and a microwave oven. Taro and Noriko each have a bed in their room, but their parents sleep on a **futon**, a padded mattress, in their bedroom.

During the day, the futon is rolled up and stored in the closet.

The bathroom is different from a Canadian bathroom. It has two compartments. One is for the toilet and sink. One is for the bathtub and shower. Before getting into the tub, you are supposed to soap yourself down and then rinse off. Then you climb into the tub for a good hot soaking. Since you are already clean when you get in the tub, the water does not get dirty. This way, another family member can use the tub after you without having to change the water. This is a good way to conserve water.

Some modern Japanese homes have bathrooms that have a regular tub and shower. Taro's home has a traditional bathroom. How does this kind of bath conserve water? What are some other ways to conserve water? Make a list.

SOMETHING TO DO

1. How many square metres is the tatami room in Taro's home? Draw a diagram to show how you found your answer.

2. Using the picture of the floor plan of Taro's home, answer the following questions:

   a. In which room is the television set?
   b. What do Taro and Noriko have in their bedrooms beside their beds?
   c. Would you like to live in the Hayashi house? Why or why not?

raditional Japanese food is very different from the food eaten in North America. People in Japan eat much more rice and much more fish than most North Americans do. Even the utensils used at the table are different. Wooden chopsticks serve in place of knives and forks.

It takes years of practice to learn the art of making sushi, a Japanese dish that combines raw fish or vegetables with sticky rice.

Japanese Diet

Other foods 40%

Rice 60%

1950

Japanese Diet

Rice 28%

Other foods 72%

1990

These charts show that Japanese people are eating less rice than they used to. Western-style meals with meat, cheese, and eggs have become more popular. Some health experts fear that these changes in diet will lead to higher rates of heart disease and cancer.

THE MOST IMPORTANT FOOD

Rice is the **staple**, or most important part, of the Japanese diet. It is eaten at most meals, and almost every kitchen in Japan has an electric rice cooker. Japanese farmers grow thousands of different kinds of rice. In fact, half of all the available farmland in Japan is set aside to grow this one grain.

Japanese rice is very sticky. This makes it easier to eat with wooden chopsticks since the grains stick together and don't slip through the two sticks. The Japanese word for chopsticks is **hashi** (hah-shee). The person using hashi usually holds the bowl of food in the left hand

quite close to the mouth. The hashi are held in the right hand and are used to scoop food into the mouth.

FISH FOR BREAKFAST?

Another food that is eaten at almost every meal, even breakfast, is fish. Since Japan is surrounded by water, fresh fish and seafood are always available. The fish has to be very fresh because much of it is eaten raw. **Sashimi** (sah-shee-mee) is raw fish that is cut into small pieces and beautifully arranged.

Sushi (soo-shee) is a classic Japanese food that brings together raw fish and rice in one dish. The most common type of sushi is a lump of rice pressed by hand and topped by a slice of raw fish such as snapper or kingfish. Between the fish and the rice is a little dab of **wasabi** (wah-sah-bee), a very hot green mustard made from horseradish. Another kind of sushi is wrapped in **nori,** which is dried seaweed. There are thousands of sushi restaurants in Japan. Most sushi is reasonably priced, but sushi from very rare fish can cost hundreds of dollars for a single serving!

JAPANESE RESTAURANTS, OLD AND NEW

At many traditional Japanese restaurants, you can see what your food will look like even before you go inside. In the front window there are wax replicas or copies of the different dishes on the menu. They are painted very skillfully to look just like real food. Inside, the floors are covered with tatami mats and the customers sit cross-legged at low tables.

During a traditional meal, all of the food is served at the same time. Many different little bowls cover the table. Each dish should contain something to represent the land, the air, and the sea. To make the food even more attractive, some dishes are decorated with flowers made out of vegetables. Japanese cooks believe that the sense of sight is just as important as the sense of taste when enjoying a fine meal.

Not all Japanese restaurants serve traditional food. Many North American food chains can be found in today's Japan, and many children prefer a hamburger and french fries to sushi. The Japanese diet has also changed to include more dairy and meat products than in former times.

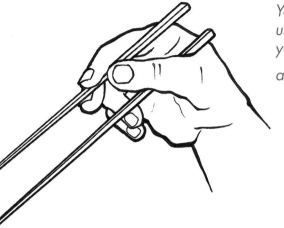

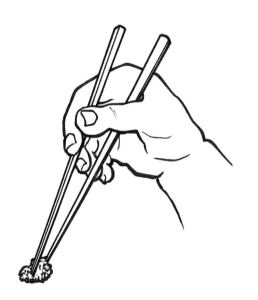

You may be an expert at using a fork but how are you with chopsticks?

a) Hold chopsticks in hand as shown. Use the hand that you normally write with. The thumb should be holding the top stick between the middle finger and the index finger. The bottom stick should rest on the ring finger.

b) When you pick something up, move your fingers to bring the top stick toward the bottom stick. The bottom stick should not move.

Wax displays like this are found in the windows of many Japanese restaurants. What kinds of food are being advertised here?

SOMETHING TO DO

1. Follow the instructions on how to hold chopsticks properly. Once you have mastered it, challenge your friends to this game. You will need several pairs of chopsticks, two large bowls, one bag of uncooked rice, and some small objects, such as candies or pennies. You will also need a timer.

   - Put the small objects into one bowl.
   - Fill the bowl three quarters full with rice, covering the candies.
   - Give each person 30 seconds to remove as many objects as possible using the chopsticks.

Today most Japanese people wear clothes similar to those worn in North America. School children wear regular play clothes and carry a special backpack for their belongings. Most high school students have to wear a school uniform. Business people always wear suits to work. Some companies, especially factories, have a uniform with the company logo on it. Traditional sports like kendo and judo have special uniforms too.

These high school students wear a school uniform. The design of the uniform varies from school to school.

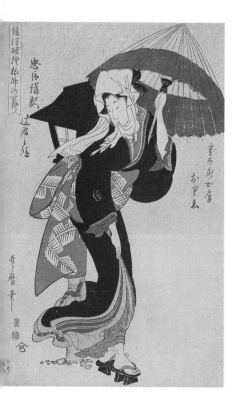

*This Japanese print shows a girl in a traditional kimono. There are no buttons or zippers on a kimono. You can see the **obi**, or sash, around the girl's waist. This is what holds the kimono together. On her feet she has heavy wooden clogs called **geta**.*

The **kimono** (kee-moh-noh) is an ancient and traditional Japanese garment. A thousand years ago it was worn for everyday use by everyone in Japan: men, women, girls, and boys. The finest kimono were made of pure silk. They were modeled on robes worn by the Chinese. Silk kimono were richly decorated and expensive to make. They were symbols of wealth and power.

Today, kimono are usually worn in public only on special occasions such as festivals and weddings. Although beautiful, the kimono that is designed for women to wear during festivals is not very comfortable. The mate-rial is heavy. The obi makes it hard to breathe. The narrow opening at the bottom allows only for little steps. It is also difficult to lift the arms, to sit, or to bend over. Cleaning one of these kimono can be tricky and time consuming. Usually the kimono is taken apart, carefully washed, and then sewn back together.

There is another type of kimono designed for casual wear around the house. Older Japanese people find these loose fitting garments to be more comfortable than Western-style clothing. Cotton kimono designed for casual wear in the summer are called **yukata** (yoo-kah-tah). Heavier flannel kimono for winter wear are called **nemaki** (neh-mah-kee).

The decorations on kimono are meant to reflect the seasons. A kimono decorated with peony flowers would be worn in the summer. One decorated with bright red maple leaves would be worn in the fall. The most expensive kimono are still made from silk. Sometimes patterns are **embroidered** or sewn on the fabric. Sometimes dyes are used to make the patterns. Today a few designers are using computers to create new designs for the kimono they manufacture.

This kimono is designed for a wedding.

SOMETHING TO DO

1. Art Activity: make a paper kimono. Follow the directions below.

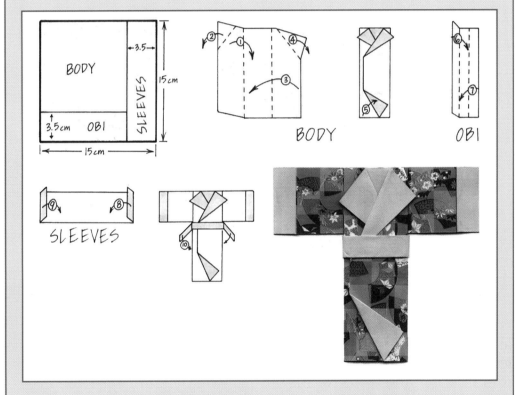

a. Glue a solid-coloured and a patterned sheet of 15 cm. x 15 cm. origami paper together.
b. Cut out the body, sleeves, and obi as shown.
c. With the solid-coloured side facing up, fold the body into thirds lengthwise and fold back the top corners to create a "collar" (steps 1 to 4 in the illustration).
d. Fold up the bottom corner of the top layer of the kimono (step 5).
e. Fold the obi into thirds lengthwise so that there are three layers (steps 6 and 7).
f. With the sleeve pattern facing upwards, fold over 1 cm. at each end. Glue in place (steps 8 and 9).
g. Glue or tape the sleeves to the back of the kimono so that the tops are even. Wrap the obi around the body with ends overlapping behind. Glue or tape in place (step 10).

ducation is very important in Japanese society. Almost 94% of all students complete high school. Japan has one of the highest **literacy** rates in the world. About 99% of the Japanese people can read and write. Noriko and Taro's parents want them to study hard. They want them to get a good job in a big company some day. Big companies usually only hire students from the best universities. To go to the best universities, students must go to good high schools. These schools have very difficult entrance exams. Taro is in grade 5 in a class of almost 40 students. This chapter outlines a typical school day for him.

Taro arrives at school with his friends. This is a typical elementary school in Japan. It has a large sand-covered playground, indoor gym and outdoor swimming pool. How does it compare with your school?

Look at the pictures below.
1. Who bows more deeply, the teacher or the students?
2. How do the boys bow? How do the girls bow?

Wearing shorts, a white shirt, and a vee-neck sweater, Taro leaves home for school. He goes to the corner and waits for his friends. They walk to school as a group like most students. They do this every week day and every other Saturday. On Saturdays school finishes at noon.

Taro arrives at school on time. Being punctual is very important at both school and work in Japan. Taro and his friends take off their shoes in the genkan and put them in wooden boxes along the wall. Then they put on either slippers or indoor tennis shoes. At the back of the classroom, he and the other boys put away their black leather backpacks. The girls put away their red ones.

At 8:30 a.m., Taro and his classmates are sitting at their desks talking excitedly and laughing. The teacher does not mind. She walks to the front of the class and says, **"Ohaiyo gozaimasu"** (oh-high-yoh goh-zai-mah-soo). That means, "Good morning". The students stand up and say, "Ohaiyo gozaimasu" as they bow.

Now they sit down to begin the daily morning meeting. For about 15 minutes, the class discusses the picnic they will have next week. They are going to a nearby mountain park. The teacher asks what games they would like to play at the park. The students are happy and excited, so some forget to put up their hands before replying. At 8:45 a.m. classes begin.

In Japanese class, Taro practices reading and writing his own language. He should know 1076 Japanese characters when he finishes grade 6 next year. In high school, he will learn old Japanese and Chinese characters as well. Every Monday Taro and his classmates do **calligraphy**, or writing practice.

Taro also has one period every day for arithmetic. Science and social studies are other important subjects for Taro and his fellow students.

At lunchtime, two students go to the kitchen and bring back a cart with trays of hot lunches for their classmates. The meal includes either bread or rice, a big main dish, vegetables, soup, and juice or milk. Everyone eats the same food. This way children cannot compare lunches. A few times a year, they must bring **bento**, or box lunches. Their mothers have to make these lunches very carefully, because the teachers sometimes check them. They should look nice and have several kinds of healthy food.

After lunch and recess, everyone helps clean the classroom. Each group has a job to do, so the work is finished quickly. They move the desks, sweep, mop floors, and clean the

blackboards. One group goes outside to do gardening. The children laugh because they enjoy working together.

Next, they move their desks into a U-shape for **Ethics** class. They discuss Japanese values and how to be a good citizen. At 2:35 p.m., the teacher has a closing meeting. They talk about any problems they had during the day and tomorrow's homework. It's Monday so now the students go to a school club activity like sports, music, or art.

At 3:45 p.m., Taro goes home for a snack. Later tonight his mother will help him with about 1½ hours of homework. He does not have time to play today, because his violin lesson is at 4:30 p.m. Next year, Taro might go to a private **cram school** two or three times a week. Cram schools give students extra training in subjects like Math and Japanese.

What kind of materials is the girl using to do brush calligraphy?

SOMETHING TO DO

1. How does Taro's schedule at school compare with your own? Make a two-column organizer to compare your school schedule with Taro's.

Celebrating a Shinto festival often involves participating in a special dance.

n Japan, the two major religions are Shinto and Buddhism. Every neighbourhood has a Shinto **shrine** and usually a Buddhist **temple.** Many Japanese follow both Shinto and Buddhism.

This statue in Kamakura, Japan is called the **Daibutsu** or "Great Buddha."

SHINTO

The word **Shinto** comes from a Chinese term meaning "the way of the gods." It is the most ancient religion in Japan. Shinto teaches that there are spirits called **kami**. These spirits can be found in living things such as animals, or non-living things such as mountains and rivers. This belief in nature spirits is one reason why Japanese people have such a strong respect for the natural world. Shinto also teaches respect for ancestors, especially for your parents. Ceremonies that celebrate life are often Shinto; for example, weddings, graduations, and births. Shinto is **unique** to Japan. That means it is not practiced elsewhere.

BUDDHISM

Buddha means "one awakened to truth." The man who came to be known as the Buddha was born in India in the 6th century B.C. Buddhism spread from India into China and Korea. Korean monks introduced the Buddha's teachings to Japan in the 6th century A.D. Buddhist monks seek for wisdom through **meditation**. This involves sitting quietly for long periods and keeping focused on a single thought or idea. In Japan ceremonies dealing with death and the afterlife are Buddhist, for example, funerals and prayers for one's ancestors.

A TRIP TO A SHINTO SHRINE

Next month Noriko Hayashi has a set of difficult exams to write. To help prepare for them, she wants to go to a Shinto shrine to pray. The Hayashi family decides to drive to a shrine that is famous for helping students with their exams.

After parking their car, the family walks under a **torii**, a big red gate. Passing through the torii helps to purify people visiting the shrine. During seasonal festivals the shrine is crowded with people, but today it is a beautiful, peaceful place.

To the left of the entrance is a large water basin. Everyone picks up a bamboo cup with a long handle. They dip the cups into a fountain of cool, clean water and drink a little. Then they pour the water over their hands. Before praying at the shrine, hands and mouths must be clean.

Noriko walks over to a small hut on the right of the gate and buys a wooden **prayer plaque**. The priest gives her a marking pen, and she begins writing on the blank side of the plaque. She asks the gods to help her pass her exams. Then she hangs the plaque on a metal frame near the outer shrine.

A path leads directly from the gate to the outer shrine in the centre of the grounds. The priests conduct ceremonies here. On special occasions, other people can enter the building. Taro and his family walk up a few steps and stand in front of a big wooden box. They each toss a coin into the box. This money will be used to support both the shrine and the priests who live there.

Then they tell the gods that they are present by pulling on a

thick rope attached to a large bell. Taro looks up as it rings loudly twice. The Hayashis clap their hands twice, hold them together and bow their heads. Silently, they pray that Noriko will pass her exams.

Taro likes to read his fortune. In front of the shrine, on the left, there is a container with sticks in it. Taro runs over, pays some money, picks up the container, and shakes it until one stick falls through a tiny hole. The number on the stick is 17. Taro looks at the numbered boxes along the wall. When he finds box 17, he takes out a long, white strip of paper. The paper says that he will have bad luck this week, so he folds the fortune lengthwise and ties it to a statue of a lion. He hopes the spirits in the wind will blow the bad luck away.

*This is the **butsudan**, or Buddhist family altar in the home of the eldest son of a family. His wife places offerings of fresh food and drink in front of it daily. She lights incense, a stick that gives off a sweet smell when burning. Then she prays for the spirits of her husband's ancestors.*

SOMETHING TO DO

1. Which of these objects or events are Buddhist? Which are Shinto?

   a __ a wedding ceremony   d __ a family grave

   b __ a shrine   e __ a statue of Buddha

   c __ butsudan   f __ kami

2. Make a diagram of the grounds of the shrine. For example, draw a rectangle for the parking lot. Draw a much larger rectangle for the grounds. What else did the story describe? Add them to your map.

There are many festivals and holidays in Japan. Some of them come from the Shinto religion. Others came over from China and Korea and have their roots in Buddhism. Some are celebrated in the country, and others in the cities. Some Japanese festivals are very much like those celebrated in North America.

During summer festivals, Japanese people often wear flowery hats, knotted ropes, or head-bands. They believe these head-pieces give them strength and clear-thinking.

New Year's presents!
Even the little baby
Holds out her tiny hands.
—Issa

COUNTRY AND CITY FESTIVALS

In the countryside, village festivals are often related to the growing cycle of rice. In spring villagers pray for a good growing season. In autumn they give thanks for an abundant harvest. These festivals stress the relationship between people and the gods.

City festivals are usually held in the summer. Originally, people used these festivals to seek protection from disease and pests. Now they stress relationships between human beings. They usually include traditional dancing, seasonal food, and lots of fun! The most famous city summer festival is Kyoto's **Gion Matsuri** (gee-on mat-soo-ree).

SHOGATSU—CELEBRATING THE NEW YEAR

What do you do on New Year's Eve? Japanese people think that **Shogatsu** (sho-gat-soo), the celebration of the New Year, is the most important of the annual holidays. Ways of welcoming the New Year differ slightly from place to place in Japan. Everywhere, however, it is a time for getting together with other family members.

Towards the end of December, the family begins to clean their house or apartment. Then they decorate it for the New Year. First they hang a sacred rope of straw with strips of white paper over the front door. This shows that the god of the New Year is living in that house. The rope also stops bad spirits from entering. Some people also hang a sacred rope on the front bumper of their cars for a few days or weeks. Families often put small tree branches beside the entrance to their home. They believe that the god of good luck who lives in certain kinds of trees can rest there.

On the first three days of January, most government offices and companies are closed. New Year's Eve and the first day of January are usually spent visiting Shinto shrines or Buddhist temples with family. Then, in the early morning, the Emperor publicly prays for the country. On January 2, the public is allowed to enter the inner palace grounds. Most people spend January 2 and 3 making formal visits with relatives, business acquaintances, and friends. They give and receive special postcards with best wishes for the coming year. Children receive small gifts of money.

BON—ANCESTOR FESTIVAL

From July 13 to 15, the Japanese honour the spirits of their ancestors by celebrating **Bon**. This Buddhist festival is the second most important annual event. People travel long distances to be with their family during this time.

Before the festival begins, family members clean their ancestors' graves and set up a spirit altar in their home in front of the Buddhist family altar. Then most families hang a paper lantern in the window so that the spirits can find their way home. On July 13, they build a welcome fire. For three days, the family leaves special offerings by the altar. These include food such as fresh fruits, vegetables, and **mochi** (moh-kee), a special kind of rice cake. They also give the spirits something to drink, such as water, rice wine, or juice. The family burns strong-smelling incense sticks and prays for their ancestors' souls. Sometimes a priest from the family shrine visits their home to say prayers also.

The festival ends with a good-bye fire on July 16 to help the spirits find their way back to the spirit world. Many people light paper lanterns and set them adrift on lakes or rivers. In this way they say farewell to their ancestors' spirits.

HANAMI—CHERRY-BLOSSOM VIEWING

For **Hanami** (hah-nah-mee), Cherry-blossom viewing, people of all ages gather in parks and on castle grounds. Schools and companies often hold picnics under the blossoms. Sometimes traditional dancers and musicians entertain the crowds, but often people bring portable **karaoke** (kah-rah-oh-keh) machines to entertain themselves.

Cherry-blossom viewing has always been a popular subject in Japanese literature, dance, music, and art. Now radio and television stations regularly give reports as the blossoming season gradually moves northward. They let people know where to find the best blossoming trees.

Bon is also known as the Lantern Festival.

Cherry-blossom viewing is one of the most popular spring events in Japan.

The cherry blossoms!
They have made the daimyo
Get down from his horse.
—Issa

SOMETHING TO DO

1. What kind of Canadian festivals and holidays do you know about? Make a list of all the holidays you can think of. Now choose one to write about. Write a brief essay explaining what you usually do on this holiday. Explain why you like this holiday so much.

I n Japan three widely celebrated festivals focus on children. All Japanese children look forward to these festivals with intense pleasure. The children's festivals are organized around the numbers three, five, and seven.

This family has a beautiful display of dolls dressed in their ancient costumes. Objects that are passed on to family members through generations are called **heirlooms.** *What heirlooms does your family have?*

This pair of dolls!
Taking them out of the box,
I remember their faces.
—Buson

Carp kites are displayed outside of this Japanese home.

HINA MATSURI — THE DOLL FESTIVAL

The first of the festivals occurs on March third, the third day of the third month. It is called **Hina Matsuri** (hee-nah mat-soo-ree) or the Doll Festival. It was originally a festival for girls in Japan so it is also known as Girls' Day. Today the whole family celebrates.

Many families in Japan have a collection of 15 dolls that represent the Emperor and Empress and their court. Some of these dolls can be hundreds of years old. They have been handed down in the family from generation to generation.

Each doll is handmade and is dressed in beautiful silk clothing. The dolls are displayed only during this festival. They are placed on a special doll stand with seven shelves covered in felt. The Emperor and Empress always have the honoured position on the top shelf. The stand also holds finely crafted miniature flowers. The edges of the stand are decorated with real peach blossoms. Peach blossoms, a symbol of beauty and happiness, are in bloom at this time of year. Girls dress up in their best kimono and visitors come to see the doll displays and to enjoy tea and **hisimochi** (hee-see-moh-kee), diamond-shaped rice cakes.

KODOMO-NO-HI — CHILDREN'S DAY

The second children's festival occurs on May 5, the fifth day of the fifth month. This festival was originally known as Boys' Day. Outside each house, carp kites were flown on bamboo poles. (The carp is a large and powerful freshwater fish.) Each kite represented one son. Today all family members are represented by carp kites. The older the family member, the larger the size of the carp. The carp was chosen as a symbol because it has to swim upstream against the current to lay its eggs. This takes great strength. It is this strength and determination that Japanese parents hope to pass on to their children. The carp is a good example to follow.

Some children display their Samurai dolls and armour on Children's Day. This is also a time to visit friends. Some communities have public wrestling matches, cultural dances, games and competitions for all to participate in.

SHICHI-GO-SAN

Shichi-Go-San takes place on November 15. Translated it means "seven-five-three." All children who are three years of age, boys who are five, and girls who are seven participate in this festival. In the morning the girls dress in their best kimono and the boys dress in their best suits. They carry **chitose ame** (chee-toh-seh ah-meh), thousand-year candy. This kind of candy symbolizes long life. The children go to shrines with their families to receive blessings from the spirits and to thank them for their help in the past. Children ring a large bell and clap their hands to attract the attention of the spirits. Then they pray for health, happiness, and long life. After a visit to the shrine, families go home to have parties. The children receive presents and treats.

Children wear their best outfits for Shichi-Go-San. What are some occasions that you must dress up for?

SOMETHING TO DO

1. Create your own carp kite! You will need one large piece of tissue paper, one pipe cleaner or other piece of strong wire, some tissue paper scraps of other colours, a glue stick, scissors, and string.

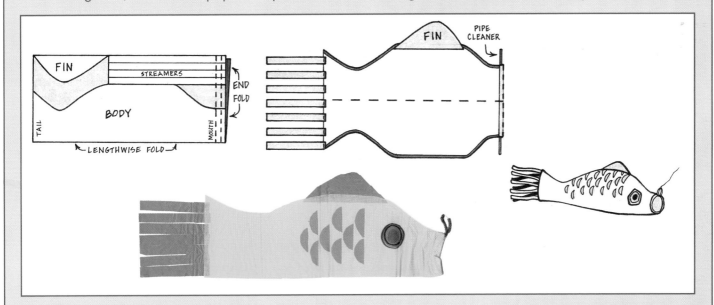

a. Using a large sheet of tissue paper, fold one end over twice, about 2 cm. each time. Turn paper over so that the "endfold" is underneath.

b. Fold the sheet in half lengthwise with endfold inside.

c. Cut out fish shape without cutting fold at bottom. The mouth must be at the endfold.

d. Unfold the body and glue the fin to the top and the streamers to the tail.

e. Unroll the endfold and place pipe cleaner inside. Refold and glue in place.

f. Refold the fish body in half and tie pipe cleaners together into a loop.

g. Glue the top edges of the body together.

h. Decorate with eyes and scales using scraps of colourful tissue paper.

i. Shape the mouth into a circle by bending the pipe cleaner. Tie a string to the outer loop and hang.

artial arts are methods of fighting first developed by the samurai warriors. The samurai took these arts very seriously. For them it was a matter of life and death. They had to be able to defend themselves and defeat their opponents. Today the martial arts are practiced as sports. All of the martial arts develop both physical strength and mental toughness. Some martial arts teach the use of different weapons, and some teach self-defense without weapons.

Judo has been an Olympic sport for more than 30 years. What Olympic sports do you enjoy practicing?

These children are learning kendo during lessons after school. Many children participate in this martial art to stay fit. What do you do to stay fit?

FIGHTING WITHOUT WEAPONS

Judo

Judo, which means "the soft way," is a method of self-defence without weapons. In some ways it looks like Western-style wrestling. Judo teaches you how to overcome your opponent by using his or her strength to your own advantage. The most common move in judo is the "throw." To throw someone correctly, first you have to yield to their attack. Then you use their energy to throw them to the floor.

Today judo is a way for people to keep fit and healthy and also to develop mental discipline. Many judo students start their training by learning **kata** or forms. Each kata is a series of slow movements that practice different techniques of attack and defence. Judo students wear a **gi** (gee), a uniform of loose-fitting pants and a jacket made of strong cloth. The jacket is fastened with a belt. The color of the belt identifies the rank of the student. Beginners wear white belts and judo masters wear black belts. Students between these two ranks wear belts of different colours.

Karate

Karate, like judo, is a form of unarmed martial art. The study of karate was developed on the Japanese island of Okinawa in the 17th century. It was very popular with the peasants who were not allowed to own weapons. They had to learn to defend themselves using only their hands and feet.

Karate students learn how to concentrate all their strength at the point of impact of a punch or kick. They train hard to toughen up the different parts of their body that form the striking surfaces. These include the knuckles and outer edge of the hand, the ball and heel of the foot, and the elbows and knees. Karate masters can break a pine board several inches thick with one blow. In ancient times, they had to be able to outfight an opponent wearing armour!

As with judo, karate teaches that mental toughness and respect for your teachers are just as important as physical skill.

FIGHTING WITH WEAPONS

Japanese Sword Fighting

Kendo, Japanese fencing, is one of the martial arts that trains students to use a weapon. The samurai warriors developed sword fighting into a science. Today, people who participate in this sport wear protective equipment that is like the samurai's armour. Even while practicing, kendo students have to wear a thick, long robe, a face mask, gloves, and a breastplate. They use steel swords only for tournaments or exhibitions. When practicing they use long bamboo sticks. This way they will not be cut by the sharp edge of a steel sword. Players receive points for striking their opponent

on the throat, head, upper body, or wrist. All of these body parts are protected by padded coverings. At the end of the match, the player with the most points wins.

Archery

Kyudo, which means "the way of the bow," is Japanese archery. A very long bow is used to shoot razor-sharp arrows. At one time, samurai archers took target practice on horseback. They used live animals as targets. Today, participants shoot from a standing position. They try to hit a target that is about 40 centimetres wide from a distance of about 30 metres. Even though it is important to hit the target, judges also look for good form. The archer has to be standing straight up with his or her arms held properly in relation to the bow.

Kyudo archers use a bow that is over 2 metres in length. How much taller than you is the bow?

SOMETHING TO DO

1. Survey your class on the physical activities that they participate in. Create a bar graph to show how many of your classmates participate in each sport.

2. Ju-do means the soft way. Bushi-do means the warrior's way. Kyu-do means the way of the bow. Can you guess what ken-do means?

Taro is very excited today. His father is taking him to a **sumo** wrestling tournament. Sumo wrestling is Taro's favourite spectator sport. He has watched it on television since he was a baby. This is the first time Taro will see the sport "live." When Taro and his father get to the hall, they find the stands are already packed with people. Luckily Taro and Mr. Hayashi have tickets for reserved seats. In many countries there are national sports. In Canada it is hockey. In the United States it is baseball. In Japan the national sport is sumo wrestling.

Here is a sumo match in progress. The wrestler gets a good grip on his opponent's belt. Then he tries to push him out of the ring or knock him off balance. The referee watches to make sure the wrestlers fight fairly. Most sumo wrestlers weigh more than 130 kilograms. The heaviest in history weighed about 260 kilograms.

The first thing Taro and Mr. Hayashi see is the **dohyo iri** (doh-yoh eer-ee), or "ring-entering ceremony." This ceremony is part of the **ritual** or set of traditional actions that are always performed before the wrestling begins. First the wrestlers purify themselves by washing their hands and rinsing their mouths. Then they clap their hands to attract the gods. Slowly they stamp their feet to drive evil spirits away from them. At the end of the ring-entering ceremony, both wrestlers sprinkle salt over the dirt wrestling ring to purify it.

Once the match begins, each wrestler tries either to push his opponent out of the ring or to force him to the ground. Wrestlers are not allowed to touch the ground with any part of their body except the soles of their feet. The matches are usually very brief, lasting only a few seconds. Usually the ring-entering ceremony takes longer than the match itself.

Look at the picture of the sumo wrestlers. Notice how heavy they are, especially around the hips and thighs. This kind of body gives them great strength for pushing heavy weights.

To gain the tremendous amounts of weight they need, sumo wrestlers eat a high-protein diet. This means they eat the kinds of food that build muscles and pack on body fat. One of the

Sumo Wrestling and Baseball

basic foods for a sumo wrestler in training is a stew called **chanko nabe** (chan-koh nah-beh). This stew contains loads of meat and fish as well as vegetables and **tofu** (toh-foo) or bean curd. The wrestlers also consume bowl after bowl of rice and drink glasses of beer. The younger sumo wrestlers have to eat enormous servings to gain as much weight as possible. The older wrestlers are already at their desired weight and can eat less.

There are several hundred professional sumo wrestlers in Japan, but only a few **Yokozuna** (yoh-koh-zoo-nah) or grand champions. While Taro watches the sumo wrestlers battling in the ring, he dreams of someday becoming a Yokozuna himself.

BASEBALL

Baseball has been played in Japan for more than 100 years. It was introduced to the Japanese by American missionaries, people who went to Japan to preach the Christian faith. Baseball is so popular in Japan that sometimes you must book a field two months in advance to play a game.

People in Japan don't just watch baseball games on television, they play every chance they get. One in ten Japanese belongs to an amateur baseball league. The Senior High School Baseball Championship has been played for the past 75 years. Every spring, high school students from all over Japan participate.

Japan also has many professional baseball teams. Just as Canadians and Americans enjoy watching the World Series, people in Japan tune in to see the Japan Series at the end of the baseball season. The team that wins becomes **Nihon-ichi** (nee-hon itch-ee), number one in Japan.

The Japanese people have also adopted other foreign sports that are gaining in popularity. Golf is very popular, especially with business people. Because of the shortage of land, many golfers can only go to a driving range. Joining a golf club is very expensive in Japan. Some people pay almost a year's wages to join one of these clubs. Tennis, volleyball, skiing, jogging, and other sports are also popular.

Baseball is a popular spectator sport in Japan. What is your favourite sport?

Sumo wrestlers eat a diet that is heavy in protein. Make a list of different kinds of foods that add protein to the body. Do you like these foods yourself? Why or why not?

SOMETHING TO DO

1. Have you ever been to a professional wrestling match or baseball, football, soccer, or hockey game? In groups, choose one professional sport. Write the name of the sport across the top of a piece of paper. Below, make a two-column organizer. Label one column, "Things we liked about the game and why." Label the other column, "Things we disliked about the game and why." Fill in both columns.

   When you are finished, answer this question: Would you like to go to another game? Why or why not?

2. When you went to the game was there any kind of ritual that took place before the game started? If so, identify the ritual. Why do you think this takes place before every game?

*J*apanese can be a difficult language for non-Japanese people to learn. This is because it has one of the most complex writing systems of any language in the world. Also, there are three levels of politeness in spoken Japanese. You would say the same thing in different ways to your friend, to a stranger, and to someone of great importance to you. Let's take a closer look at the way Japanese people communicate.

Can you guess what these gestures mean in Japan? Match the number to the picture. Then show what gestures you use for the same meanings.
1. Come here!
2. Money.
3. Me

Bowing is an important form of body language in Japan. People bow on meeting to show respect for each other.

BODY LANGUAGE

People use more than words when they communicate. There is also something called **body language**. By moving your head, by leaning forward, by looking bored or excited, you can show what you are thinking without using words. People can also use gestures, or hand movements, while they are speaking. Just as Japanese words are different from English words, the body language also differs between people in Japan and people in North America.

Most Japanese people do not make large gestures with their hands while they are talking.

Society expects them to show self-control. Many people, however, nod often and make listening sounds to encourage the speaker to continue. The listener may also say "Yes" regularly or repeat the speaker's key words to show interest.

On the whole, Japanese people are more comfortable with long silences in conversation than North Americans are. In Japan, silence shows that the speaker is taking time to think carefully before saying something. On the part of the listener, silence is a sign of politeness and of respect for the other person's views.

Speaking and Writing Japanese

LEVELS OF SPEECH

There are three levels of speech in the Japanese language:
- informal
- formal
- very formal.

When you speak to someone younger than yourself, you use the informal level. You also use this level when speaking to members of your "in-group," such as family and close friends. You use a formal level of language for in-group members who are older than you. Anyone you do not know very well is also spoken to formally. Finally, you use the very formal level of speech if you are speaking to your teacher or to a customer or your boss at work.

How do you switch from an informal to a formal level of speech? In Japanese, this is done mostly by changing the endings of the **verbs** or action words you use. Also, formal speech uses many more terms of respect than informal speech does. This happens in English, too. For instance, you sometimes address a stranger as "Sir" and use the word "please" when asking a question. In Japanese, however, there are many more words that show respect for the person you are addressing.

NAMES

In Japan, the family name comes before the first name. Imagine you were friends with Noriko Hayashi. In Japan you would call her Hayashi Noriko, not the other way around. A visitor to Japan whose name was Jane Smith might be called Smith Jane.

Only Noriko's closest friends and family members would call her "Noriko." They might also call her "Noriko-chan," which means "little Noriko" or "Noriko dear" to people close to her.

When Noriko grows older and enters the business world, people will address her as "Hayashi-san." The word **san** shows respect for Noriko. **Sensei** (sen-say) is used instead of San when speaking to teachers, politicians, doctors, or other very important people. Sensei originally meant "a person born before me."

Taro Hayashi has to switch back and forth between the three levels of spoken Japanese many times each day. When Taro talks with his friends, he uses the informal level. When he asks an older person for directions, he uses the formal level. When Taro speaks to his teacher in class, he uses the very formal level of speech and calls the teacher "Sensei."

WRITING JAPANESE

The Japanese writing system is complicated because there are three different scripts or ways of writing words. In one of these scripts, the Japanese use difficult symbols called **kanji** (kan-jee). These are explained below. Just imagine how much more difficult English would be if you had to learn three different alphabets before you could write a sentence.

JAPANESE CHARACTERS (KANJI)

Kanji are **characters** or written symbols that the Japanese have borrowed from the Chinese writing system. Long, long ago, these Chinese characters looked like small pictures or drawings of different things. They have changed over the years so that most of them do not look like pictures anymore. Each kanji stands for a single word or idea. They are used for writing the main parts of speech, such as nouns and verbs, and descriptive words such as adjectives and adverbs.

In Japan, children begin learning simple kanji in grade one. By the end of high school, they have to be able to read and write almost 2000 of these characters.

When they were first written down thousands of years ago, kanji were simple pictures of different things in nature. Below are some of the simplest and most common kanji.

one **ichi**	two **ni**	three **san**	human **hito**	man **otoko**	woman **onna**

river **kawa**	mountain **yama**	tree **ki**	woods **hayashi**	sun **hi**	rain **ame**	gate **mon**

Can you see the river flowing between its banks in the kanji for **kawa**? Can you see the three mountain peaks in the kanji for **yama**? In the kanji for **ame**, can you see the raindrops? Some kanji can be combined to make new words. When two trees are placed beside each other, this becomes the word for "woods."

OTHER JAPANESE CHARACTERS

Even though there are thousands of kanji, there are not enough to show all the words in the Japanese language. This is because Japanese has a different kind of grammar, or sentence structure, than Chinese, the language that first used the kanji symbols.

When they are writing, the Japanese have to mix kanji characters with two other sets of symbols. The first is called **hiragana** (hir-ah-gah-nah). These are for Japanese words and parts of words for which there is no kanji character.

The third set of Japanese characters is called **katakana** (kah-tah-kah-nah). These symbols are used for "loan words" that come into Japanese from other languages. Today there are many English loan words in the Japanese language. Here are some of the most common loan words. In the first

column they appear as they are pronounced in Japanese. In the second column is the English "translation."

jiinzu	jeans
naifu	knife
hoteru	hotel
erebeta	elevator
hanbaga	hamburger

In Japan, "X" means wrong and "O" means correct. In the centre of the blackboard, you can see the right and wrong way to write the kanji that means both moon (tsuki) and month (gatsu). In the box on the right, this kanji has been combined with another to write a new kanji in yellow chalk.

SOMETHING TO DO

1. What kinds of body language do English speakers sometimes use? Demonstrate.

2. Make a Japanese scroll. Using a brush and black paint, copy onto it all the Japanese characters you can find in this chapter.

3. With a friend, practice saying these common Japanese words, expressions, and greetings.

Hai (High)	Yes.
Iie (Ee-eh)	No.
Domo (Doh-moh)	Thanks.
Do itashimashite (Doh ee-tah-shee-mash-teh)	You're welcome.
Ohaiyo gozaimasu (Oh-high-yoh goh-zai-mah-soo)	Good morning.
Konnichi wa (Koh-nee-chi wah)	Good afternoon.
Konban wa (Kon-ban wah)	Good evening.
Sumimasen (Soo-mee-mah-sen)	Excuse me.
O genki desu ka? (Oh gen-kee deh-soo kah)	How are you?
Hai, genki desu (High gen-kee deh-soo)	I'm fine.

As with many other countries, Japan has its share of legends, myths, and folk tales. Many of these stories were first told by the elders in a village hundreds of years ago and then passed down through generations of a family. Later the stories were written down and recorded. Japanese legends, like legends from other countries, were often based on real-life people and historical events.

This Japanese print shows the 47 ronin attacking Kira's fortified palace. Why do you think this story became legendary in Japan?

LEGENDS

In the story of the 47 ronin, the Shogun appointed Lord Asano to receive three ambassadors. An official named Kira was supposed to advise Lord Asano about the best way of dealing with the ambassadors. Instead, Kira insulted Lord Asano on many occasions. Finally, Lord Asano had enough. In the Shogun's palace, he drew his sword and wounded Kira. The Shogun sentenced Lord Asano to death by suicide and seized the lord's property.

After Lord Asano killed himself, 47 of his warriors became **ronin,** wandering samurai with no leader. They swore to avenge their lord's death. For two years they made their plans. Finally they attacked Kira's fortified palace, broke inside, and killed him. All but one of the 47 ronin escaped. Later they surrendered, and the Shogun ordered them to commit suicide.

These events actually happened in Japan around 1700. Soon they became the subject of plays and paintings. Each artist added something to the story or changed the facts in some way to make the story even more exciting. Before long the deeds of the 47 ronin had become a **legend**, a traditional story that was handed down from age to age.

JAPANESE MYTHS

In most myths the characters are gods and goddesses. You may be familiar with some Greek myths that tell stories about the gods Jove and Apollo and the goddesses Athena and Hera.

The Japanese people have their own myths. One of them explains how the islands of Japan were created. The creator god chose two young gods, Izanagi and his beautiful companion Izanami, to bring beauty to earth. As they descended to the lifeless planet, Izanagi thrust his spear into the fog that surrounded them. Soon the fog cleared and the sun shone. Mud flowed from the tip of the spear to create the first island of Japan. Then water flowed to surround the new land. Eventually the other islands were created and the two young gods populated the earth with their children. The first emperor of Japan is said to have been the great grandson of Izanagi and Izanami.

Izanagi creates Japan with his magic spear. How did this story affect the Japanese people's view of the emperor?

SOMETHING TO DO

1. Go to the library and find a book on Japanese legends. Choose a legend you like. After reading the legend carefully, tell it to the rest of your class. Is the legend easy or hard to remember? Why?

FOLK TALES

A **folk tale** is a simple story with a moral or lesson to teach. Many folk tales have animals as characters. Goblins and ogres often appear to play their tricks. A folk tale usually has a surprise ending. The following story follows this folk tale format.

How To Fool a Cat

Once upon a time there was a rich daimyo who liked to collect carvings of animals. He had many kinds, but he had no carved mouse. So he called two skilled carvers to him and said: "I want each of you to carve a mouse for me. These mice must be so lifelike that my cat will think they're real and pounce on them. We'll put them down together and see which mouse the cat pounces on first. To the carver of that mouse I'll give this bag of gold."

The two carvers went back to their homes and set to work. After a time they came back. One had carved a wonderful mouse out of wood. It was so well done that it looked exactly like a mouse. The other, however, had done very badly. He had used some material that flaked and looked funny. It didn't look like a mouse at all.

"What's this?" said the daimyo. "This wooden mouse is a marvelous piece of carving, but this other mouse wouldn't fool anyone, let alone a cat."

"Let the cat be brought in," said the second carver. "The cat can decide which is the better mouse."

SOMETHING TO DO

1. Folk tales often teach important lessons. What was the lesson in the story of the carved mice?

2. With a group of friends, act out or mime this story. You could also make puppets and put on a puppet show.

The daimyo thought this was rather silly, but he ordered the cat to be brought in. No sooner had it come into the room than it pounced upon the badly carved mouse and paid no attention at all to the one that was carved so well.

There was nothing for the daimyo to do but give the gold to the unskillful carver. As he did so he said, "Well, now that you have the gold, tell me how you did it."

"It was easy, my lord," said the man. "I didn't carve my mouse from wood. I carved it from dried fish. That's why the cat pounced upon it so swiftly."

When the daimyo heard how the cat and everyone else had been fooled, he could not help laughing, and soon everyone in the entire court was holding their sides with laughter.

"Well," said the daimyo finally, "then I'll have to give two bags of gold. One to the workman who carved so well, and one to you who carved so cleverly. I'll keep the wooden mouse, and we'll let the cat have the other one."

Literature, the art of poetry and stories, can be traced back to very early times in Japan. The oldest Japanese stories and poems were often based on forms developed by Chinese writers. Stories often focused on the emperor's court, and poems on the four seasons and the beauty of nature. Over the years, the Japanese developed their own forms of literature. The most famous of these is a type of poetry called haiku.

This print shows a Japanese village at nightfall under deep snow. Like the artists who made such prints, haiku poets tried to create a mood by capturing a single moment in time. After you have read through this chapter, see if you can write a haiku about the winter scene in this print.

HAIKU POETRY

Haiku is a very short kind of poem. Most haiku follow strict rules. Usually the poem is written in three lines. The first line contains five syllables, the second contains seven, and the third five. This adds up to a total of 17 syllables.

Here is a Japanese haiku to show you how the poem is organized. First the haiku appears in Japanese characters. Then the characters are translated into Roman letters to show how they are pronounced. Can you count the syllables? Beneath is an English translation to give you the meaning of the poem. Because of the difficulty of translating Japanese into English, the English version sometimes does not contain exactly 17 syllables.

春雨や猫に踊を教へる子

一 茶

Harusame ya
Spring rain is falling.
neko ni odori wo
The little girl is teaching
oshieru ko
Her kitten to dance.
—Issa

The content of the poem also follows certain rules. In most haiku there will be a "season word." Sometimes this will be the actual name of one of the four seasons: winter, spring, summer, or fall. At other times it could be the name of a holiday, such as the New Year. Since the New Year falls on January 1, the reader knows that the poem's season is winter. At other times, the poet may refer to a type of insect, such as a mosquito. Since mosquitoes are most active during the summer months, this would be a summer haiku. What is the season word in the haiku above?

Since haiku are so short, they usually focus on a single action or event. Usually the poet also mentions the natural world. This reflects the great respect the Japanese people have for nature. The haiku poet tries to get the reader to feel a certain mood or emotion.

What is happening in the poem about the girl and her kitten? It is raining so hard outside that the little girl cannot go out to play. She turns to the family cat for company and decides to teach it to dance. We see a picture in our minds of the little girl holding the cat by its front paws and talking to it. The cat may be trying to run away. Outside the rain is beating all around the house. How does this make you feel?

SOME HAIKU POETS

Basho was the most famous of the haiku poets. We read about him in Chapter 4. Basho wrote what is probably still the best-known haiku in the world.

Ah, the ancient pond.
Suddenly a frog jumps in.
The sound of water!

Issa was another famous writer of haiku. Like Basho, he was very poor for most of his life. When his father died, Issa was cheated out of his inheritance. He wandered around Japan writing poetry and leading a very simple life. When he was 51, he won back some of the money that had been taken from him. He bought a small house and married. Still his problems were

not over. His first four children all died as babies, and his wife died in childbirth. Through all of this Issa continued writing poetry. He had a special concern for poor people. He also wrote many poems about insects.

O fleas!
For you too the night must be long.
It must be lonely.

Many women also wrote haiku. Here is a poem one woman wrote on the Doll's Festival.

Ah, the dolls' faces!
Although I didn't mean to,
I have grown old.
—Seifu

HAIKU TODAY

Today haiku writing is still very popular in Japan. There are many magazines that publish nothing but haiku and there are several contests each year for the best haiku on different subjects. In the twentieth century, haiku also became popular with poets in the West.

SOMETHING TO DO

1. Write your own haiku following the steps outlined below.

   - Think of a season.
   - Think of a single event or picture to write about.
   - Now write your haiku in three lines. Make the second line longer than the first and third.
   - Let your haiku "sit" for a day or two. Look at it again. See if there is anything you want to change about it to make it better. Rewrite your haiku.
   - Share your haiku with other members of your class. Read theirs as well.

Here is a Japanese scroll showing a haiku by a modern poet. The poet has eaten blowfish sushi. This is a great delicacy in Japan. If the fish is not prepared properly, though, it can be poisonous. In English, the haiku reads:

I ate a blowfish.
Waking up in the night,
I think: Will I die?

Japan has developed its own kinds of drama. These are very different from plays in North America and Europe. Three ancient forms have remained popular in today's Japan. In **Noh** (no) drama, the actors wear wooden masks and mime their parts. In **Kabuki** (kah-boo-kee), the actors wear heavy make-up and traditional clothing. **Bunraku** (bun-rack-oo) uses large puppets to tell the story.

The scenery in Noh theatre is often very simple. In this way the audience finds it easier to focus on the decorated masks and costumes.

NOH THEATRE

Noh is the oldest form of theatre in Japan. It was first developed in the fourteenth and fifteenth centuries. In the past, Noh actors performed for the nobility and samurai warriors. The lower classes were not allowed to watch. Today everyone can enjoy this form of drama.

In a Noh play, the story is narrated by a **chorus**, or group of singers, on one side of the stage. The scenery is very plain, often just a painted screen at the back of the stage. The actors mime their roles and at times perform dances. They wear wooden masks to show their inner feelings. If they are happy, they wear smiling masks. If something terrible happens, they put on frowning masks. To accompany the actors and the chorus, four musicians play different kinds of drums and a flute. The stories told in Noh drama are based on Japanese folk tales and legends. They often show the way a person's fortune can quickly change. Someone who is a millionaire today can become a poor person tomorrow.

Most Noh plays are quite short, usually lasting 20 minutes or so. An evening at a Noh theatre will usually include three Noh plays. In between the plays actors perform short comic sketches.

This Noh mask is made of wood. What emotion is it meant to suggest?

Kabuki uses a combination of dance, music, sound effects, an orchestra, and a chorus. Some people in the audience participate by yelling and cheering. Since the plays are so long, people in the audience often bring meals and eat them while watching.

KABUKI

Kabuki is another form of traditional Japanese theatre, but it is very different from Noh. Instead of being designed for the nobility, Kabuki was meant to be enjoyed by the lower classes. Perhaps that is why in Kabuki the hero is often a clever peasant, and the villain is a greedy and dim-witted noble. Kabuki plays are also much longer than Noh plays, some of them lasting more than six hours. As many as 50 actors will participate.

Kabuki plays are funny, but they also teach important lessons.

PUPPET THEATRE

Bunraku are plays acted out by large, almost life-sized puppets. The puppeteers move the puppets to Japanese music as the narrator tells the story. The puppeteers can be seen on stage, but since they wear all-black clothing the audience is not distracted by them. The puppets are so large that three puppeteers are needed to move each one. Today robots and computers also help move some of the puppets.

All of these forms of ancient Japanese theatre are very popular in Japan today. At the same time, there is a busy theatre community in Japan that performs modern plays. Many of these plays are translations of works by Western playwrights. Others are written by Japanese playwrights about present-day Japan.

The puppeteer's skill brings the puppets to life on stage as the story is told.

SOMETHING TO DO

1. Design a mask for a character or emotion of your own choice. You can create a great mask using plaster casting, which is available in most craft supply stores. Follow the instructions carefully and get an adult to help. Cardboard, paper plates, and construction paper can also be used to make a Japanese theatre mask.

2. Go to the library to find a Japanese legend. Working in a group, act out the legend in mime. See if you can find some traditional Japanese music to play in the background while your group acts out the legend.

Art is very important in Japanese culture. Many Japanese homes have a **tokonoma**. This is a space set in the wall of a room. A painted **scroll** (a long piece of paper) and a flower arrangement are displayed in the space. Both the scroll and the flowers change with the seasons. In this way the people in the house feel more in tune with nature, even if they live in a big city.

Like many other Japanese arts, sumi-e painting has strict rules. Artists must learn how to paint simple things first, such as blades of grass. Only after much practice can they go on to paint something as challenging as this waterfall scene.

PAINTING

Sumi-e painting is a very old art form. The word sumi-e means "black-ink picture." Instead of paint, the artist uses black ink and a special brush to create a picture of something found in nature. The artist paints on rice paper and must work very quickly. Mistakes cannot be erased because the delicate paper will tear. If the artist's hand shakes even a little the ink will smear. Every stroke of the brush must be perfect! Most sumi-e artists focus on plants and animals in their paintings.

FLOWER ARRANGING

Japanese flower arranging is called **ikebana**. It was developed during the eighth century when people presented flowers to the gods as an offering. The flowers are arranged in a special way to show the harmony between nature and humanity. The arrangement also focuses the viewer's eye on the natural beauty of the flowers.

First, a long-stemmed flower is placed in the middle of a low pot. Then a shorter flower goes on either side. The tall flower in the middle stands for heaven. The next tallest stands for human beings. The shortest flower represents the earth on which we live. Taken together, the three flowers symbolize the whole universe.

In an ikebana arrangement, the flowers will often be in different stages of bloom. Full blooms symbolize the past. Blooms that are just opening symbolize the present, and unopened buds stand for the future.

The kinds of flowers used in ikebana change with the seasons. In spring, branches

Here is a picture of an ikebana arrangement. Which of the flowers in this arrangement represents heaven? Can you tell which season these flowers are meant to represent?

from flowering fruit trees, such as cherries and plums, are used. In summer, garden flowers appear, and in fall dried grasses and chrysanthemums. Winter arrangements show bare branches or pine and cedar boughs.

THE TEA CEREMONY

Japanese Buddhist monks first developed the tea ceremony. These monks needed something to keep them awake while they meditated. During **meditation**, a monk had to sit cross-legged for hours with his mind fixed on a single thought.

Today the tea ceremony is performed by one person for as many as five guests. It is important to hold the ceremony in a peaceful place. Often the tea room is separated from the main house and set in the garden. In smaller houses and apartments, it is simply a separate room. The door to the tea room is usually quite small, so that the guests have to bend over as they enter. In this way they show humility and respect for their host.

The ceremony is always performed in the same way. First the guests wash their hands and mouth and remove their shoes. The tea room always contains a tokonoma. The guests admire the flower arrangement and scroll in the tokonoma as they enter the tea room.

Then the host brings in the cups and tea pot on a special tray. When the coals in the pit are hot enough, the water is put on to boil. While they wait, the guests are served traditional sweets, which often are made to look like flower blossoms. When the water boils, the host makes the tea by whisking tea powder

into the hot water. Since no sweetener is used, the tea usually tastes bitter. Each guest has to drink the tea in exactly three-and-a-half sips.

After drinking the tea, the guests admire the beautiful tea cups. Then the dishes are collected and washed. The tea ceremony is meant to bring about a soothing state of mind in the host and guests. It does this by stressing the following four qualities: cleanliness, respect, harmony, and peacefulness.

Created by Buddhist monks, the Japanese tea ceremony is still practiced today.

SOMETHING TO DO

1. Follow the examples below to create your own sumi-e painting. You will need a paint brush and black ink.

2. If you live in a city with a Japanese cultural centre, invite someone from the centre to class to demonstrate the tea ceremony. What part of the ceremony do you like the best? Why?

Song and dance are ways of communicating and celebrating one's culture. As with many other arts in Japan, Japanese song and dance are a mixture of the traditional and modern forms. Taro likes to listen to rock music, but he also spends hours practicing the **taiko** (tie-koh), the traditional Japanese drum.

The **koto** (koh-toh) is one of the oldest of the traditional Japanese instruments. It has 13 strings and sounds something like a lute.

There are many kinds of traditional music that play an important role in Japanese theatre, seasonal festivals, and religious ceremonies.

TRADITIONAL MUSIC

Much traditional Japanese music sounds strange to Western ears. This is because Japanese musicians have different ideas about **harmony** and **melody** than do musicians in the West. The melody of a song is its tune; harmony is the way the different instruments blend together in a particular song. Another reason Japanese music sounds different is that it is played on instruments that are unique to Japan.

FOLK SONGS

Japanese folk songs praise the beauty of nature and the four seasons. People sing **Sakura**, a well known traditional song, in honour of the spring cherry blossoms. **Haru ga Kita** is another such song that elementary school children all across Japan sing.

CONTEMPORARY MUSIC

Singing karaoke (kare-ee-OH-kee) and listening to live or recorded music are probably the most popular ways to relax in Japan. This is true for people of

HARU GA KITA (Springtime Has Come)

Ha - ru ga ki - ta. Ha - ru ga ki - ta. Do - ko ni ki - ta?   Ya - ma ni ki - ta.
(hah-roo gah kee-tah.   hah-roo gah kee-tah.   doh-koh nee kee-tah.   yah-mah nee kee-tah)
Springtime has come.   Springtime has come.   Where has it come?   It's come to the mountains.

Sa - to ni ki - ta. No - ni mo ki - ta.
(sah-toh nee kee-tah.   noh-nee moh kee-tah.)
It's come to the village.   It's also come to the fields.

all ages. Karaoke, singing along to pre-recorded background music with the lyrics on a TV screen, was invented in Japan.

Ryuichi Sakamoto (roo-ee-chee sah-kah-moh-toh)

Orange-dyed hair is one of the trademarks of the Japanese music composer Ryuichi Sakamoto. He is also a world-famous actor, author, and producer. He combined his interest in electronics and world music by studying "electronic and ethno music" at the University of Tokyo. The group he formed after graduation broke new ground in the use of synthesizers in pop music in the 1980s and in the "rave" music heard in dance clubs worldwide in the 1990s.

DANCE

Most of Japan's traditional dances began in ancient times as part of religious ceremonies. Today these dances are divided into two main types. **Mai** (mahee), which is associated with the Noh theatre, and **Odori** (oh-doh-ree) which is sometimes seen in Kabuki plays.

Mai is the Japanese word for "revolving." The young girls who worked in Shinto shrines developed this form of dancing. In a typical mai dance, one or two performers will circle a stage

while holding an umbrella or fan or some other prop. The movements are slow and stately.

Odori means "jumping." It developed out of Buddhist ceremonies in which the monks would ring bells and jump about in time to the music. When kabuki plays became popular, the actors began to dance in this fashion. The movements in odori dancing are more free and less formal than in mai dancing.

Today there are many Japanese dance troupes that specialize in modern forms of dance. Many of these focus on Western styles of dance such as ballet. Others combine traditional Japanese dance movements with Western styles.

The **Awa Odori** (ah-wah oh-doh-ree) Festival in Tokushima, on the island of Shikoku, takes place every August. It is one of the three biggest festivals in Japan and centres around dancing. The dancers are accompanied by drums, bamboo flutes, shamisens, and singers.

Sakamoto's music for the movie, The Last Emperor, won him a British Academy Award, an Oscar, and a Golden Globe award for "best original score."

SOMETHING TO DO

1. Brainstorm some names of Canadian music groups and musicians. Name kinds of music they play. What kind of music do you like/dislike? Why? How does it make you feel when you listen to it?

2. Listen to different kinds of traditional Japanese music. Describe how the tempo, rhythm, and melody work together to express a mood. Draw an emotion line as you listen to different kinds of music.

 n the past, the emperor or the shogun ruled Japan. The emperors were **hereditary** rulers. That means the right to rule was passed to them through their family. The shoguns were military rulers. They came to power by defeating their enemies in battle. After World War II, Japan became a **democracy**. In a democracy the people choose their leaders by voting in an election.

The Diet meets in this building in Tokyo, the capital of Japan. The members of the Diet are elected by Japanese citizens. In Japan, all citizens who are 20 or older can vote in elections.

THE GOVERNMENT OF JAPAN

What Is a Constitution?

A **constitution** is a set of rules that describes how a country is governed. It tells about the rights and duties of the people. For example, people in Japan have the right to freedom of speech and freedom of religion. At the same time, they have the duty to pay taxes and obey the law.

The current Japanese constitution went into effect on May 3, 1947. It set up a form of government very similar to that in Canada. In Japan the national legislature is called the Diet instead of Parliament as in Canada. The Diet is the group of elected officials who pass new laws for Japan. Japan also has a prime minister to lead the government. The prime minister has a cabinet, or a group of trusted officials, to offer advice and help.

Who Is the Emperor?

Until 1945, people believed the emperor had supernatural powers that allowed him to communicate with the gods. He was a high priest of the Shinto religion. Throughout most of Japan's history the shogun had the real power in Japan. The emperor was more like a **figurehead** or symbolic ruler. This changed in the period of Japanese history known as the **Meiji** period (1868 to 1912). The samurai grew unhappy with the shogun. In 1868, they took away his power and gave it to the emperor.

After World War II (1945), the emperor's role in politics and society changed. On New Year's Day 1946, the Emperor Hirohito declared that he was not a god or high priest. Today, the emperor's role is symbolic only. The people show great respect for the emperor, but he does not take a direct role in running the government. The present emperor, Akihito, is the 125th emperor of Japan. He and his wife, Empress Michiko, have three grown children: Crown Prince Naruhito, Prince Akishino and Princess Sayako.

JAPANESE SOCIETY

Japanese society has changed much over the last 50 years, and it is still changing in many ways. Many Japanese, however, still hold traditional values about the way people should behave. For most people in Japan, the group is still more important than the single person. People are expected to work not just for themselves, but for the good of their family, of the company they work for, and of Japanese society as a whole.

In general, most people in Japan try not to show their negative feelings (such as anger or frustration) in public. In an effort to be polite, people may not say exactly what is on their mind. Sometimes when two Japanese people are talking, each one has to try to "read between the lines" to find out what the other is really saying. Each person has to listen carefully to the other person's tone of voice. It also helps to watch for slight changes in facial expressions or hand gestures.

Let's look at one example. If a Japanese friend asked you for a favour, you would try to avoid saying something like, "No, I can't do that." Many people in Japan would consider a direct refusal like this to be rude. Instead, you might say something like, "I will do my best." Your tone of voice or the look on your face might tell your friend that the answer is "No." However, your friend's feelings are not hurt in the way they would be if you simply said, "No way!"

In Japanese society there are still different **status** levels. Each person's status depends on their age, job, family background, and the level of education they have

Only members of the Japanese royal family can become emperors, usually the eldest son.

reached. Younger people are usually expected to show respect for their elders. Students are supposed to respect their teachers.

There are other ways of showing what a person's status is in Japan. If you work in a group office, something like the placement of your desk can show your status. A senior employee's desk may be set off on its own and have a nice view by a window. The desk of a junior employee may be jammed in with several others in a place where there are no windows.

SOMETHING TO DO

1. In Japan, the emperor who used to lead the government now plays a symbolic role. The Queen of England plays a similar role for Canada. Make a list of the ways in which the Queen acts as the symbolic head of government in Canada.

2. Working with a partner, brainstorm some rules for table manners in Canada. Make a list. Which of these rules seem important to you? Which do you think are unimportant? Why?

tudy the photos of Japanese cities below. What things in the pictures look as if they belonged to traditional Japan? What things look modern? For example, the lanterns look traditional, but the library looks modern. Which photo is related to the future?

Candy store.

Library.

Construction site.

Ameyoko market in Tokyo.

Castle.

Cities in Japan offer a startling mixture of the old and new. You might see a small rice field next to a tall office building. A punk rocker with spiky, orange-coloured hair brushes past an elderly woman selling fish from a wooden cart. You can watch traditional Kabuki, Bunraku, and Noh theatre or the latest movies from around the world. Everywhere you turn, the past and the present exist side by side. You can see a glimpse of the future in construction sites for new buildings and in the changing attitudes of the young people.

In the 1880s, Japan began to **industrialize**. This means it began to rely more on factory work than on farming to support its economy. Gradually, people who had been living on farms in the country began moving to cities, which were the centres of industry. They moved in hopes of making more money and living a better life.

In Japan, each city is made up of many districts. Each district can be quite different. Even a huge city like Tokyo can feel like a number of small towns that have been put together in one place.

Modern, flashy shopping areas and business districts in the big cities are usually crowded. In the residential areas, where people have their homes, it is not as crowded. These areas often have narrow, winding streets.

In the older cities, neigh-bourhoods are named after the class of people who used to live there. These cities will have neighborhoods with names like Merchant Town, Priest Town, and Samurai Town.

Many old Japanese cities still have a castle or the ruins of one. The castle will usually be surrounded by a deep moat with water in it. The neighborhood around the castle will have very narrow streets that wind back and forth in a confused pattern. Can you guess why this is so?

Tokyo

In 1992, Tokyo, the capital of Japan, became the world's largest city. When the surrounding towns and urban areas are included, Tokyo has a population of more than 26 million. Twenty-one per cent of all the people living in Japan live in Tokyo.

Tokyo is located on the wide Kanto Plain. This is the largest area of flat land in Japan. The Tokyo urban area has spread out until now it takes up almost this entire plain. It is surrounded by mountains on three sides and by Tokyo Bay on the fourth. So Tokyo cannot continue to grow by spreading outwards. Instead, it has begun to spread up and down. Engineers have found ways of constructing tall buildings that can withstand earthquakes like the one that levelled

Tokyo in 1923. Also, they have begun building many underground shopping malls and entertainment centres. Every bit of available space is being used.

Cost of Living in Tokyo

A survey done in 1995 compared prices in Tokyo, New York, London (England), and Paris. Tokyo was the most expensive city for food, clothes, shoes, and other goods and services. A kilogram of rice in Tokyo costs about twice what you would pay for it in Toronto. As well as being the largest city in the world, Tokyo is also one of the most expensive!

In 1870, many more people in Japan lived in the country than in the cities. By 1980, most Japanese lived in cities. This reflects Japan's move away from an economy based on farming to one based on manufacturing.

Population

1870

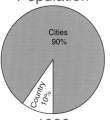

Population

1980

SOMETHING TO DO

1. Make a bar graph to compare the size of Tokyo, Osaka, Sapporo, Toronto, Vancouver, and Montreal using the information you find in an atlas or encyclopedia.

2. Look at the population pie charts on this page. Suggest reasons to explain why more people in Japan want to live in the city than in the country. Where would you rather live? Why?

*J*apanese people work at many of the same occupations that we have in North America. There are businesspeople, teachers, firefighters, engineers, postal workers, musicians, and artists. Some obvious differences also exist between Japan and North America in the way that jobs are organized.

A supervisor leads workers through their morning exercise routine at a farm machinery factory. This is a common practice in many large Japanese corporations.

One of these differences is the **seniority system.** The longer a person works for a company the more the company rewards that person. In some ways this is good, but the system also has its drawbacks. Consider Mr. Seito. He has worked at the same company for 16 years. During that time he has not developed many new skills. Mr. Ichimada works in the same department as Mr. Seito and has been with the company for 15 years. He has worked very hard at acquiring new skills and developed into an excellent employee. When the head of the department retires, Mr. Seito is automatically promoted to fill the position even though Mr. Ichimada is more qualified.

Another unique aspect of the Japanese employment system is **lifetime employment**. This has been a feature of large companies since the end of World War II in 1945. Lifetime employment gives workers job security by promising that they can work for the same company until retirement. In return, they must be willing to work overtime and transfer to other departments, cities, or countries. Employers expect their workers to be very loyal and to consider work more important even than their family.

A **recession** hit Japan in the early 1990s. During a recession companies have trouble making enough money to stay in business. The recession caused many companies to take a hard look at the seniority system and lifetime employment. Some companies began to make seniority less important than talent, skill, and hard work. Since the recession, it is possible for younger people to be promoted before their seniors. Also, some companies no longer practice lifetime employment. People who are getting high salaries but not working hard enough may be "bullied" into quitting their jobs. Men aged 45 to 54 have become Japan's fastest-growing group of unemployed.

Mr. Hayashi's Work Day

6:00 A.M. Mr. Hayashi's clock radio wakes him up. For the next 45 minutes he rushes to get ready for work. He has a quick breakfast, then walks to the train station, 15 minutes from home.

7:00 A.M. The train always arrives right on time, but it is also always packed with people. Mr. Hayashi is on the train for an hour and a half. He uses that time to read company reports and plan his day.

8:45 A.M. After a short walk from the train station, Mr. Hayashi arrives in his office. His day is filled with desk work and long meetings.

1:00 P.M. Mr. Hayashi has lunch. Some days he has lunch at his desk while he continues to work. Other days he takes business clients out for lunch.

8:30 P.M. Mr. Hayashi begins the long trip home. He was finished his work by 7:00 p.m., but he doesn't like to leave the building before his boss goes home.

10:15 P.M. When Mr. Hayashi arrives home, he finds his wife, Yuka, waiting up for him. There is a hot supper ready, but his children have already gone to bed. During the week he rarely sees Noriko and Taro except for a few rushed minutes in the morning.

Mrs. Hayashi's Work History

Until recently, women in Japan were not expected to have a lifetime career outside the home. Many of the jobs that were open to women offered little chance of promotion. When Yuka Hayashi graduated from university, she worked as an "office lady." Although Yuka was good at accounting, she spent most of her time typing, answering the phone, and making photocopies. After she married and had her first child, Yuka was encouraged to quit her job. Now Yuka works as a full-time mother and homemaker.

Today, it is more common for Japanese women to have careers outside of the home. Changes in the workplace have also meant that more women are working as managers and supervisors.

Most large Japanese companies use the "open office" concept. Employees work at desks with several fellow-workers. Only some upper management employees get a desk or an office to themselves.

SOMETHING TO DO

1. Talk in groups about the advantages and disadvantages of the seniority system and lifetime employment as practiced in Japan. Make a list of the points your group discovers. Share your list with other groups.

25

Today Japan is an economic superpower. In fact, it has one of the largest economies of any country in the world. This is a great achievement, especially since the country was in ruins at the end of World War II. In the 50 years following the war, the Japanese have enjoyed spectacular success in the three areas of industry, technology, and trade.

This robot is nicknamed "Waseda legs" because it was developed at Waseda University in Tokyo. In the future, it may help legless people walk.

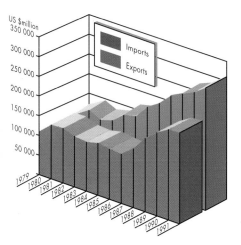

This graph shows the value of Japan's exports and imports between 1979 and 1991. Since 1981, Japan's exports have been worth more than its imports.

INDUSTRY

In the 1950s and '60s, Japanese companies focused on heavy industries such as steel, cement, and chemical production. Each of these products is made from **raw materials** that Japan has to **import** or buy from other countries. Steel is made from iron ore, cement from clay and lime, and many chemicals can be made from petroleum. As the price of these raw materials rose higher and higher in the 1960s and '70s, manufacturing companies in Japan began to lose money. For this reason, some Japanese companies shifted their focus from heavy industries to lighter ones. These included the making of automobiles, cameras, and electronic supplies.

TECHNOLOGY

Soon other countries in Asia, such as Korea, began to compete against Japan in world markets. Korea succeeded in marketing a line of cars that competed directly with the sale of Japanese cars. Again, Japanese companies adjusted, this time in two ways. First, they began to concentrate on making **high technology** products such as computer chips and compact disks (CDs). Secondly, the companies improved their factories so that they could produce their items more quickly and cheaply than their competitors.

One way the Japanese have improved their factories is through the use of more **robots**, machines that can be used to replace human workers. Robots are often used in car factories, especially for such jobs as welding the steel frames. Since the robots can work faster than the people they replaced, the cars are cheaper to produce. Thanks to their robots, Japanese companies can sell their cars at competitive prices around the world. They can also sell their robots! Japan has become the largest producer and seller of robots in the world.

Industry, Technology, and Trade

TRADE

Japan still has one of the largest petroleum refining industries in the world. It is also one of the world's largest producers of steel and cement products. To supply the factories that make these products, Japan has to import great quantities of expensive raw materials. In 1989, for instance, the Japanese had to import 90% to 100% of the following materials for use in their factories: petroleum, copper, coal, iron, lead, nickel, cotton, wool, and rubber.

How does Japan pay for these expensive raw materials that it imports in such large quantities? The answer is that Japan exports or sells to other countries many more goods than it imports.

THE ENVIRONMENT

Many of Japan's factories are located near the water that surrounds the country. This makes it easy for ships carrying raw materials to deliver them directly to the factories. This in turn saves time and money. Although the location of Japan's factories has benefits, it has also caused some harm. Some factories have dumped their harmful chemicals into the water. Japan has suffered from high rates of water and air pollution, especially in large cities like Tokyo. This pollution has threatened Japan's fishing industry and the health of its people. More recently, Japan's Diet has passed a number of anti-pollution laws.

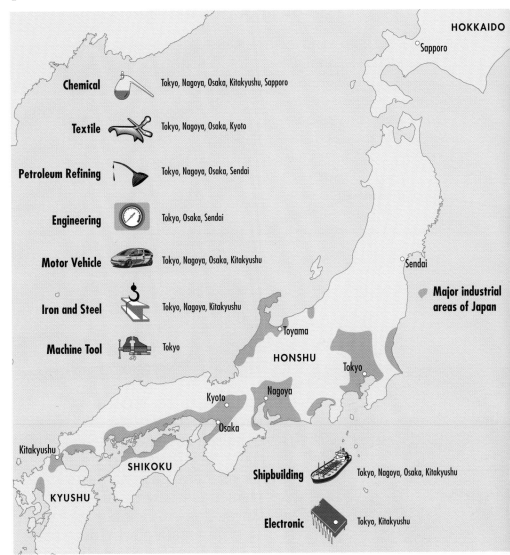

Industry	Cities
Chemical	Tokyo, Nagoya, Osaka, Kitakyushu, Sapporo
Textile	Tokyo, Nagoya, Osaka, Kyoto
Petroleum Refining	Tokyo, Nagoya, Osaka, Sendai
Engineering	Tokyo, Osaka, Sendai
Motor Vehicle	Tokyo, Nagoya, Osaka, Kitakyushu
Iron and Steel	Tokyo, Nagoya, Kitakyushu
Machine Tool	Tokyo
Shipbuilding	Tokyo, Nagoya, Osaka, Kitakyushu
Electronic	Tokyo, Kitakyushu

Major industrial areas of Japan

SOMETHING TO DO

1. Work with a group of three other students. Each student should bring to class some magazines that contain advertisements. As a group, look through the magazines to find logos for products that are made in Japan. Working together, make a collage displaying the logos.

2. Whales, sea otters, cod, and some types of salmon are endangered species. Research one species of sea animal or fish to find out more about it. Answer the following questions:

   - why did it become endangered?
   - what is being done to protect it?
   - what more could be done? Be specific in your answers.

26

*J*apan has one of the world's best transportation systems. Despite the mountainous terrain, speedy railroads and good highways link Japan's larger cities and towns. Every major city has its own subway system. People also use bicycles, cars, buses, taxis, airplanes, ferry boats, and hydrofoils as other means of dependable travel.

It is important for there to be good transportation between the four main islands of Japan. Many ferry boats carry people between the islands. Here a ferry boat leaves the island of Shikoku for Honshu. Check the map on page 2. Which of these islands is larger?

It is not unusual in Japan to see uniformed "people pushers" shoving commuters onto subway trains. In this way every bit of space on the trains is used.

GETTING TO WORK AND SCHOOL

How do you get to school each day? Taro Hayashi rides his bicycle to his neighbourhood elementary school. His sister, Noriko, has to ride her bike to the train station and then travel for 30 minutes to her junior high school. Her commuter train stops about every 5 minutes, so it is rather slow. It takes her father one-and-a-half hours in each direction to **commute** to work. Sometimes he has trouble finding a seat because the train is really crowded during rush hour. In fact, **people pushers** are paid to shove riders into the train!

A TRIP TO SAPPORO

Next week, Mrs. Hayashi and the children will travel from their home in Osaka to Sapporo on the northern island of Hokkaido. They are returning to Mr. Hayashi's childhood home for the Bon Festival. Mr. Hayashi will fly to Sapporo, since he can only take three days off for the holiday. He will arrive in about 2 hours and 30 minutes. His family will travel for more than 13 hours. Mrs. Hayashi wants her children to travel by land so that they can see the different parts of their country.

So, on August 11, they will travel by **Shinkansen**, or bullet train, through Kyoto and Nagoya to Tokyo. This first step of the journey will take 2 hours and 56 minutes. Taro can't wait to get on the Shinkansen because these trains are the fastest form of land transportation in Japan. Taro is also happy because he knows his mother will buy him a delicious bento (boxed lunch) on the train. After arriving in Tokyo, the Hayashis will change bullet trains and go on to Morioka, where the Shinkansen line ends. It will take them three-and-a-half hours to travel between Tokyo and Morioka.

From Morioka, the Hayashis will take a two-and-a-half hour bus ride to Aomori City. From there they could take the train through an underwater tunnel to Hakodate, but they will probably travel by **hydrofoil** instead. The hydrofoil is a boat that travels slightly above the surface of the water. At Hakodate they will take a four-and-a-half hour train ride to Sapporo. Finally, their relatives will pick them up in Sapporo and drive them to their home.

New Bullet Train Sets Speed Record

Nagoya—A new model of the Shinkansen bullet train set a Japanese speed record of 426.6 kph late Thursday during a midnight test run. Central Japan Railway Company said the 300X test model broke the previous Japanese train record of 425 kph set in December 1993 by East Japan Railway Company. The sleek six-car, 152-metre-long train conducted the test run between Kyoto and Maibara after regular service had ended for the day.

Source: Reprinted from the Daily Yomiuri, *July 13, 1996.*

SOMETHING TO DO

1. Read the article from a Japanese newspaper and answer these questions:

   - What is the name of the train?
   - Why do you think a Shinkansen is called a bullet train?
   - What is the top speed of the bullet train in the article?
   - What does kph mean?
   - How would you describe the size of the train?

2. On a map of Japan, find the major cities that the Hayashi family will travel through. On your own map of Japan, write the names of those cities in the correct places. Draw a small house where the Hayashi family lives and another where their relatives live. To map out the Hayashis' trip, draw lines connecting the cities. Use a different kind of line for each kind of transportation. For example, use a double line for a bullet train and a dotted line for a bus. Include Mr. Hayashi's flight as well.

27

After their long journey, the Hayashi family arrives at Mr. Hayashi's childhood home in the country. Mr. Hayashi's brother, Eiji, comes to pick them up from the train station in his car. When they reach the home, the whole family is there to greet them. Taro and Noriko's grandfather wants to give his two grandchildren a tour of the farm. The children learn that most Japanese farms are a little more than one hectare in area. After working for a few days on the farm, they realize that just because the farm is small does not mean that the work is easy!

Taro digs up weeds in the vegetable garden under his grandfather's watchful eye.

The small farm plots in Japan give a high yield of fruits and vegetables. Japanese farmers are able to satisfy about three-quarters of the country's food needs. Japanese technology has helped the farming industry by creating highly efficient machines, pesticides, and herbicides. This technology saves enough time that many farmers are able to hold a second job in the city. Family members help out during harvesting and planting times. Since only about 15% of Japan's land is suitable for farming, farmers also plant different kinds of crops on their fields. No space is wasted. Sometimes you can see these small and very efficient family farms in the middle of a large city.

In the cooler northern regions, farmers grow crops such as apples, tomatoes, carrots, onions, and strawberries. Tea, oranges, and peaches must be grown in the warmer climates of southern Japan. Although mixed farming is happening more and more, rice is still Japan's most important food crop. Rice is also used for many purposes. It can be made into a rice wine called **sake**. It can be mixed with soybeans and made into a thick paste called **miso**. Japanese cooks use miso to make a nutritious soup often eaten for breakfast. Tatami mats, straw hats, and sandals are made from the stalks of the rice plant.

Japanese farmers grow thousands of different types of rice. Scientists have created new types

so that farmers can grow rice all over Japan, not just in the south where it is warm year round.

Rice is grown in **paddies**. Paddies are fields that are flooded on purpose. This crop needs plenty of water, so Japan's damp climate and mild temperatures are perfect for rice growing. In many areas rice farmers grow two crops each year. The rice seeds are first planted in dry fields. When the small seedlings are ready, the farmers transplant them into the flooded paddies.

Finally, when the rice stalks are ready, the fields are drained and dried. The stalks are cut by a machine and the rice is removed from the plant by **threshing** or beating it. For many farmers, harvest time is still a time of great celebration. There are Shinto festivals to thank the gods for a good rice harvest. In the past, many believed that rice was a gift from the gods. Only the nobility could afford to eat this crop. The peasants had to eat barley instead.

The photo shows terraced rice paddies on the Japanese island of Kyushu. Using a system of terraces like this means that farmers can grow rice on hillsides. It also helps to prevent **erosion**, *the washing away of soil by wind and rain.*

SOMETHING TO DO

1. Create a resource map showing the major crops in your province. Use symbols for each type of crop, and place the symbols on the map to show where the different crops are grown. Use a legend to identify each symbol.

2. Farmers in Japan and Canada use pesticides to create better crops. Is this really better for the consumer? Working with a partner, do some research about pesticides and herbicides to find out more about the damage that they have caused and the benefits that they give. Discuss your results and together suggest other ways farmers can protect their crops from harmful insects and weeds.

or centuries Japanese art and literature have celebrated the beauty of nature. The Shinto religion teaches that there are gods or spirits present in different natural formations such as animals, trees, mountains, rivers, and scenes of great beauty. These spirits are called **kami** and act as protectors of villages and towns and the people in them. The Japanese have always had great respect for the natural resources of their land.

When the uguisu sings,
My heart is filled
With painful longings.
—Onitsura

The uguisu bird. This bird has such a sweet song that it is the subject of many poems in Japanese.

PLANT LIFE

We saw in Chapter 1 that the climate of Japan varies widely from the island of Hokkaido in the north to Kyushu in the south. This variation in climate means that Japan also has a wide range of plant and animal life. There are five to six thousand kinds of native plants in Japan. Japanese red cedar is the country's main source of timber. Other common trees include ginkgo, cherry, bamboo, and Japanese maple.

When the Japanese use wood to build their houses, they do not usually paint it. Instead they allow a stain or varnish to bring out the natural beauty of the wood grain.

The Japanese like to say that a tree has two lives: one when it is growing, and another when it forms part of a house or other kind of building.

More than 60% of the land in Japan is forested. Most of these wooded areas are privately owned, or recently planted, or belong to national parks. Since many of these trees cannot be cut down, Japan's lumber supply is growing smaller year by year. In 1994, more than 50% of the country's lumber was imported from Canada.

Plant and Animal Life

A family of fishers sort their catch for the day.

ANIMAL LIFE

Like the vegetation, the animal life of Japan differs from region to region. There are about 570 bird species found throughout the country. One of them, the **uguisu** (oo-goo-ee-soo) or Japanese nightingale, is frequently mentioned in haiku poems that celebrate the season of spring.

Other wildlife found in the mountainous areas include the Japanese antelope, the tanuki (raccoon dog), fox, flying squirrel, Japanese monkey, and rabbit. On the northern island of Hokkaido, which has cold winters with lots of snow, you can see black bear, red deer, sable, ground squirrels, hares, and other species also found in Canada.

FISHING

There are about 3000 species of fish found in the fresh and salt waters of Japan. The Japanese take great pride in the variety and beauty of their sea creatures. Seafood is more common than red meat or fowl at the dinner table. As with Japanese farms, most fishing boats are owned and operated by families or small businesses. In recent years, however, the number of people who earn their living by fishing has been decreasing. As a result, Japan has become a major importer of seafood to satisfy its people's taste for seaweed, fish, and shellfish.

SOMETHING TO DO

1. In groups, do some research to find out more about Japanese plants and animals. Then, write down five clues about one of the plants or animals. Make the first clue the most difficult and the last clue the easiest to guess. Share your clues with other groups to see if anyone can guess your plant or animal.

2. Write your own haiku about a Japanese plant or animal. Follow the steps you learned in Chapter 18.

29

Most of the early Japanese immigrants to Canada came from crowded fishing or farming villages on the islands of Kyushu and Honshu. Like many immigrants to Canada, they sought a better life. When they arrived in Canada, they settled in the coastal cities of British Columbia. There they practiced the same occupations they had known in Japan: fishing and farming.

ISSEI: FIRST-GENERATION JAPANESE CANADIANS

The first Japanese immigrants arrived in Canada in the late 1870s. These early immigrants were called **Issei** (ee-say), which is Japanese for "first generation." The Issei were born in Japan.

Unfortunately, early Japanese Canadians met with **prejudice** or suspicion in Canada. Other Canadians accused the Japanese of wanting to take away their jobs. Even though this was not true, the government of British Columbia began to pass laws that made life very difficult for the Issei.

First, the government set a limit on the number of Japanese who could come to Canada. Then Japanese Canadians were denied the right to vote. The government also passed a law that said Japanese Canadians could not become doctors, lawyers, teachers, or government workers. This meant that Japanese Canadians often had to work at the lowest-paying jobs.

NISEI: SECOND-GENERATION JAPANESE CANADIANS

When Canada declared war on Japan in 1941, conditions grew even worse for Japanese Canadians. By this time, many of the original Japanese settlers had raised children. These children, born in Canada and therefore Canadian citizens, were called **Nisei** (nee-say), or "second generation."

In 1942, the Canadian government rounded up all the Japanese Canadians living in the coastal areas of British Columbia and sent them to **detention camps**. Some of these camps were in the forests of British Columbia. Some were on farms in Alberta or Manitoba. The Japanese Canadians had to stay in these camps until the end of the war. While they were there, the government sold their homes

This photo shows a group of Japanese Canadian women and children during World War II. They are in the community kitchen of the detention camp at Slocan, B.C.

and fishing boats at low prices and then kept much of the money to help pay for building the camps.

In 1988, the government of Canada apologized to Japanese Canadians for the way they were treated during World War II. Each surviving victim of the camps received a check for $21 000 to help pay for the property they lost. The government also gave $12 million to an organization for stamping out prejudice in Canadian society.

JAPANESE CANADIANS TODAY

After World War II, Japanese Canadians set about rebuilding their lives. Today there are many Japanese Canadians who work as lawyers, doctors, teachers, artists, and entertainers. Here are two portraits of successful Japanese Canadians.

KIMIKO KOYANAGI

Kimiko spent the first 30 years of her life in Japan. There she learned traditional Japanese doll-making techniques from her older brothers and sisters. In Japan, making dolls is an ancient art form. Doll makers must follow very strict rules. Kimiko moved to Canada in the 1960s after marrying a Japanese-Canadian architect. Kimiko and her husband settled in Burlington, Ontario.

Canada does not have an ancient doll-making tradition. Here, Kimiko feels free to express more of her inner feelings in her work. Now she is creating sculptures rather than dolls. This new work of Kimiko's is a union of Japanese and Canadian art forms.

SEVERN CULLIS SUZUKI

Severn is the daughter of the well-known broadcaster David Suzuki and Tara Cullis. In 1992, when she was 13 years old, Severn gave a speech at the Earth Summit in Brazil. The Earth Summit was a meeting of officials from nations around the world. These people worked together to find solutions for world-wide environmental problems such as pollution and global warming. Severn received a standing ovation for her speech. These are a few of her words:

"I'm only a child, yet I know we are all part of a family, five billion strong; in fact, 30 million species strong. We all share the same air, water, and soil. Borders and governments will never change that. . . . I'm only a child, yet I know if all the money spent on war was spent on ending poverty and finding environmental answers, what a wonderful place this earth would be."

Here is one of Kimiko's sculptures. It is called Yume. Kimiko says this sculpture represents a young girl's dreams of the future, life, and love.

Severn Cullis Suzuki. If you were writing your own speech on environmental problems, what recommendations would you make?

SOMETHING TO DO

1. Organize a Japanese Cultural Festival. Decorate your classroom or an outdoor space with Japanese crafts. These could include carp kites, paper kimono, and information posters about Japan. Set up booths and a performance area to demonstrate skills you have learned in this book.

   Plan your festival as a class, then form small groups to prepare demonstrations in: the tea ceremony, calligraphy, crafts, dance, music, flower arranging, martial arts, and haiku writing. Invite members of the Japanese community to help you plan and demonstrate. Teach others what you have learned!

Glossary

active volcano a volcano that can erupt at any time.

atomic bomb a bomb that gets its power from the release of nuclear energy.

Awa Odori a dance festival that is celebrated every August on the island of Shikoku.

bento a wood or plastic lunch box divided into sections.

body language communication through body movements or posture.

Bon also known as the Lantern Festival, Bon is the second-most important festival in Japan after the New Year. It is a Buddhist festival in which the Japanese people honour the spirits of their ancestors.

Buddha This word means "one awakened to truth." The Buddha was born in India around 563 B.C., and his religion spread to Japan in 552 A.D.

Bunraku a form of Japanese theatre that uses large, almost life-size puppets to tell a story.

bushido the Japanese word for martial arts, the way of the warrior.

butsudan a Buddhist altar or holy place in a person's home.

calligraphy handwriting, especially when done in a beautiful style.

central vent the main passageway for lava escaping from the cone of a volcano.

chanko nabe a rich stew, heavy in protein, that sumo wrestlers eat to gain and maintain their weight.

character a written letter or symbol.

chitose ame a type of candy given to children during the Shichi-go-san festival.

chorus a group of singers who perform in a play.

commute to travel back and forth to work.

cone the mass of raised earth and cooled lava that surrounds the central vent of a volcano.

cram school a school in Japan that provides extra hours of instruction after regular schools have closed. Cram schools can be for students of any age, but they are especially common with high school students trying to get into a good university.

daimyo a noble with many samurai at his command.

democracy a form of government in which citizens choose their own leaders by voting for them in an election.

detention camp In Canada during World War II a place constructed to hold Japanese Canadians until the end of the war. Most detention camps were located either on farms or near lumber camps.

dohyo iri the "ring entering ceremony;" the brief ritual at the beginning of a sumo wrestling match.

dormant volcano a volcano that is still able to erupt, though it has not done so for a long time.

earthquake a shaking of the earth's crust brought on by pressure that builds up when two of the earth's plates scrape together.

embroider to decorate a piece of cloth with needlework.

epicentre the place where an earthquake first reaches the earth's surface.

erosion a wearing away of the earth's soil through the action of wind and rain.

ethics the study of what is right and wrong.

extended family a family that includes relatives such as grandparents, aunts, uncles and cousins, all living either in the same house or in the same neighborhood.

extinct volcano a volcano that will not erupt again.

fault a break in a plate of the earth's crust.

feudal system a way of organizing society in which the nobles are given land by a ruler in return for military service.

figurehead a leader without real power.

folk tale a popular story passed down from generation to generation. These tales often have a surprise ending.

Fujisan the Japanese word for Mount Fuji.

futon a heavy mattress rolled out on the floor for use as a bed.

genkan the small room at the front of a Japanese house where people are expected to leave their shoes.

geologist a scientist who studies the Earth.

geta traditional Japanese footwear; platform shoes.

haiku a form of poetry 17 syllables long. A haiku is meant to create a mood by capturing a single moment in time, usually with a reference to the natural world.

hashi Japanese chopsticks.

hereditary passed down from one generation to the next.

hiragana a set of Japanese symbols or characters used to write down words or parts of words for which there are no kanji characters.

gi the uniform worn by students of karate and judo.

Gion Matsuri the largest of Japan's city festivals, celebrated every summer in Kyoto.

Hanami Cherry-blossom viewing. There is no set date for this spring festival because the cherry trees come into bloom on different dates each year.

harmony a combination of musical notes that produces a pleasing sound.

heirloom a piece of personal property handed down in a family from generation to generation.

high technology advanced developments in electronics, especially in regard to computer and software design.

Hina Matsuri The Doll Festival, celebrated on May 3.

hisimochi sweet, diamond-shaped rice cakes.

hydrofoil a boat with a device that lifts the boat's bottom (hull) out of the water. This increases the boat's speed.

ikebana the art of flower arranging.

imperial government a government ruled by an emperor and usually controlling a number of countries.

import to bring foreign goods into a country.

incense a kind of spice that gives off a sweet smell when burned.

industrialize to set up industries or factories in a country or a part of a country.

Issei in Canada, first-generation Japanese immigrants.

judo a martial art that teaches self-defence without weapons. In Japanese, judo means "the soft way."

Kabuki a popular form of traditional Japanese theatre.

kami in the Shinto religion, kami is the word for god or spirit.

karaoke a kind of entertainment in which someone sings a song against pre-recorded background music.

karate a martial art in which the hands and feet are used as weapons.

kata a set of pre-arranged movements that a karate or judo student must memorize and practise.

katakana a set of Japanese symbols used to write "loan words," words that Japanese has borrowed from other languages.

kendo the art of Japanese fencing or swordplay.

koto Japanese musical instrument with 13 strings.

kyudo Japanese archery.

land reforms changes to the laws of a country that affect the ownership of the land.

latitude distance north or south of the equator, shown as equally spaced lines on a map.

lava the liquid rock that flows from a volcano.

legend a traditional story thought to have a basis in fact.

leukemia cancer of the blood.

lifetime employment a guarantee by a company that its employees can work for it until they retire.